Age a

Employ____

WHY EMPLOYERS
SHOULD THINK AGAIN ABOUT
OLDER WORKERS

Richard Worsley

A C E

B O O K S

'I look at old age as the gap between how I see myself and how others see me.'
Respondent to Age Concern England survey, 1993

© 1996 Richard Worsley
Published by Age Concern England
1268 London Road
London SW16 4ER

Editor Caroline Hartnell
Design and typesetting Eugenie Dodd Typographics
Copy preparation Vinnette Marshall
Printed and bound in Great Britain by J W Arrowsmith Ltd, Bristol

A catalogue record for this book is available
from the British Library.

ISBN 0–86242–204–3

CONTENTS

LIST OF CASE STUDIES

ABOUT THE AUTHOR

Richard Worsley was born in Kent in 1943. Educated at Ampleforth College and Cambridge, where he read law, he spent the first 12 years of his working life in the Engineering Employers Federation. His later jobs were with the Confederation of British Industry, where he was Director of Social Affairs; British Aerospace, where he was Head of Personnel; and BT, where he was Group Personnel Director and then Director of Community Affairs. He has been seconded by BT to his present job as Director of the Carnegie Third Age Programme, the follow-up to the Carnegie Inquiry into the Third Age.

He is married, with two daughters and a son. His home is on the north coast of Norfolk, where he pursues his interests in gardening, birdwatching and writing.

ACKNOWLEDGEMENTS

Although I take responsibility for the opinions and observations in the text of this book, they are derived from so many invaluable inputs from others that I have felt it appropriate to write in the first person plural.

I would like to thank all those who have participated as members of the 'Age and Employment' project (they are listed in Appendix 1) for their contributions and interest; Fred Edwards, John Naylor and Monty Meth from Carnegie for invaluable comment and suggestion as the work proceeded; Caroline Hartnell for a thoroughly professional role as my editor; Sally Greengross and Ruth Jarratt from Age Concern for their enthusiasm and encouragement. I am deeply grateful to BT, whose agreement to second me to Carnegie for three years made my involvement in this project possible. Finally, my special thanks to my wife Stephanie for her patience and support.

RTW

FOREWORD

Most large businesses in the UK have now developed equal opportunities policies which seek to outlaw workplace discrimination on
gender or race grounds; far fewer have integrated age-based discrimination into those policies. This book shows why they should now
consider so doing. It highlights the changing age structure of the UK's
workforce and explains why it is vital for companies not to ignore the
potential contribution to business success which can be made by older
workers.

I hope this will not be seen as special pleading. The issues addressed in *Age and Employment* affect every one of us in our personal
lives, and in the organisations for which we work. We will almost all
be older workers one day.

I am pleased that the Carnegie Third Age Programme has worked
so closely with Age Concern England in the project which has led to
Richard Worsley's book. Through the Employers' Forum on Age we
will be building on this work to help employers to develop positive
policies and practices in a field which they can no longer afford to neglect. The experience of those who have sought to change hearts and
minds on gender and race issues has taught that the business case
needs to be spelt out, alongside the moral case. This book does just
that for older workers.

Howard Davies
President, Age Concern England

BACKGROUND NOTE

This book originated in the Carnegie Inquiry into the Third Age – a comprehensive research programme undertaken by the Carnegie UK Trust between 1989 and 1993. The purpose of the Inquiry, which was charitably funded and politically independent, was to establish the facts, the policy options and the needs for change if the potential of those in their third age is to be fulfilled.

The 'third age' is a shorthand term used to describe a new phenomenon in our society: the emergence of a growing number of people who may have completed their 'second age' of conventional work and child-rearing and who can now look forward to two or more decades of healthy, active life before their 'fourth age' of dependency and possibly disability.

The concerns which led to the establishment of the Inquiry included the existence of widespread and unjustified age discrimination, the lack of choice for so many in their third age and the wide disparities in the circumstances of this age group, with some having improving prospects but others quite the reverse. These concerns were seen alongside the enormous potential for those in their third age to achieve personal fulfilment, experience a widening of choice, and make a major contribution to society and to the economy.

The Report of the Inquiry was welcomed and there was widespread acknowledgement of the quality of the research and its authoritative coverage of the subject. The Trust therefore decided to commission a further three-year period of work aimed at follow-up and implementation of its recommendations.

The Carnegie Third Age Programme was accordingly established for this purpose in 1993, and it was rapidly agreed that one of its most important elements would be a project to address a central set of findings and recommendations from the Report – those concerning employment.

This book is the result of that project. It was conducted with the involvement of 39 employers and other organisations who agreed to take part in their different ways – through interviews, provision of written material, 'brainstorming' sessions and comments on my text as it emerged.

The project which was established for that purpose was initially about 'employers and older workers' – as if they were a specific group of people who could be identified in terms of their age. We quickly learned, however, that we needed to look further. Age discrimination, for example, is not something which just happens to people over 50; it occurs at all ages and now affects people in their 30s and 40s as well. As our work progressed, therefore, it became more and more clear that this was not a set of issues about 'them' – a definable group of people – but about the relationship between employment and age.

1 Introduction – New lives in a new century

At the moment when the calendar turns to 2000, our lives are unlikely to change dramatically. But as we look forward to the new century, we have a chance to take stock – to reflect on the changes that we have been through and to ask ourselves how we want to plan our lives in the new era.

This book is concerned with the consequences of two huge changes which are happening now. They are of great significance for the years ahead and are often overlooked.

As we look back on the 1900s, there will be many candidates for the greatest achievement of the twentieth century. Certainly one of them must be the enormous gains which have been made in healthy life expectancy. A male child born in 1901 could have been expected to live until the age of 45, and a girl until 49. The corresponding figures today are 74 for males and 80 for females.

Whatever else the century has done for us, it has provided the prospect for each of us of three extra decades of healthy life – a prize and opportunity which our Victorian and Edwardian forebears would have been amazed to contemplate.

The second change, caused partly by the first and partly by changes in birth rates, is in the shape of our population. While the total population is steadily growing, the proportion of young people in it is dropping, the proportion of older people is rising fast, and the number of people over 80 is rising even faster. A similar pattern is reflected in the nation's workforce: there are progressively fewer people under 24 and more over 45.

Accompanying and underlying these changes has been the constant rolling forward of scientific discovery. The dramatic advances in the use of drugs, in clinical and surgical treatment and in standards of hygiene which have combined to produce that huge change in life expectancy have been matched by technological developments which have revolutionised industrial and commercial life.

But the technology which has produced those great medical and business gains has also had its impact on employment, enabling employers to achieve more output with fewer people and leading to large-scale reductions in many workforces. Employers have had to make difficult choices about whom they will retain in employment and many older people and others have been put out of work.

These are not just historic changes – they are continuing. Where will life expectancy be at the end of the twenty-first century? Will medical science deliver another similar step forward? We cannot be precise, but current developments in molecular genetics and neurobiology almost certainly mean that throughout the industrialised, advanced world many more people will be not only living well into their 80s and 90s but also physically stronger and in full possession of their mental faculties. If governments, actuaries and economists think that we have reached the end of growth in life expectancy, they could not be more wrong.

A recent French study, for example, concluded that life expectancy is now growing at the rate of one year every four years.[1] Some simple arithmetic and a little imagination will reveal the implications.

No one can sit back and ignore these changes. They will affect every single one of us and they will alter many aspects of our lives – as individuals, younger and older, as voters, in businesses and trade unions, in voluntary organisations and in Government.

There is a pressing need, for example, for all of us, workers, taxpayers, pensioners, employers and governments, to come to terms, urgently, with how to meet the income requirements of the growing number of older people – and this at a time when the number of people at work will be static or reducing. We need new ways of sharing the task of providing that income between individuals and employers and of removing hardship, poverty and fear from older people – without putting an impossible load on people at work. And if more older people are enabled to go on working, that load can be spread more widely.

We each need to develop and maintain a healthy lifestyle, and to be supported in that task, so that we can enjoy those extra years and continue to make a contribution to society, postponing as long as possible the time when we are dependent on others. Ageing is not a process which simply happens to us; it is very much influenced by the way of life we choose for ourselves, especially by our diet, the amount of exercise we take and whether or not we have an active mental life.

We need to find new ways of learning, acknowledging that the most significant assets of an organisation are likely to be intellectual rather than physical, and accepting that learning needs to happen throughout our lives, not just as a full-time process for the young but as a constant part-time activity for us all, supporting both our work and our fulfilment as individuals.

We also need to understand the implications of these changes as a growing number of very old people become dependent for care on a decreasing number of younger people. Millions are already involved in caring for older people, some in institutions but growing numbers in the home and in the family. What does this mean for carers who need and want to go on working? How are they going to get the support and respite that they need? Who will pay for residential care when staying at home is no longer possible?

We all have a real stake in these decisions. Their significance is not reduced because the changes are happening gradually. If we sit back and pretend that these are somebody else's problems, and that we can acquiesce in a constant increase in the number of people who are dependent on others, we will all – individuals and employers – pay a high price in our pensions, our benefits and our taxes. If, on the other hand, we find new ways of enabling people who want to work to do so, if we create rather than deny opportunities for people of all ages to contribute to our society and economy, we will all benefit.

This book focuses on one vital aspect of these changes – the relationship between employment and age – but in the context of all these wider questions and developments. We cannot look at work in isolation. It is a pivotal aspect of all our lives; whether or not we have it at all, how much we enjoy it, how well it is arranged – both by ourselves and by our employers – how long it lasts, how we leave it and what we do when it is finished.

Work needs to be organised and changed to accommodate the new profile of our population. It needs to reflect and to take account of the new demands and potential of a society which now, for the first time, includes a plentiful supply of healthy, experienced older people alongside those who need support in old age.

These issues are not about choosing between younger and older people. As the growth in women's employment has shown, we are not in the business of sharing out a fixed volume of work – what economists call the 'lump of labour fallacy'. They are about how different groups of people, including both younger and older people, can support and complement each other on equal terms and use their different skills, experience and potential for the common good.

There is certainly such a thing as society. If we reject the idea that we depend on each other, that we are all citizens in a community, including corporate citizens, with responsibilities which go far beyond serving our own self-interest, we are all the poorer. And just as individuals and organisations depend on each other, so do the different elements of our lives – our work, our health, our income and our knowledge.

If we can get the policies and actions right, these changes need not be threats. We have great opportunities to adapt and use new forms of work and to make the most of the talents of people of all ages.

This is a book about business issues, not a lobby for older people. Of course there is a strong case on grounds of equity and morals against age discrimination, against making unfair decisions about any aspect of people's lives simply on grounds of their age. But this book invites employers to accept that, if they decide to look positively at age in relation to employment and to adapt their businesses to the changing profile of our population, they will not only benefit all those whom they directly serve – shareholders, customers and employees – but also address their own wider interests in the health of the community and the economy.

Each of the chapters which follow concludes with a checklist of questions addressed to employers. There are no 'right answers' to these questions; each organisation will need to find its own. The aim is to help address all the issues systematically.

It is time to think again.

2 Employment and age

In this chapter, we look at one of the most important responsibilities of employers – to put together the best possible team of employees and to nurture that workforce, including their older employees. We set out the basic reasons why older workers matter to organisations, and we look at six different ways in which the face of employment is changing.

▪ Employers' responsibilities for their workforce

Chairmen and chief executives of businesses are fond of saying that their employees are their greatest asset. As the nature of companies changes, this becomes more and more true. The assets of businesses other than their employees are becoming more short-lived and of much less significance than the most important measure of real future worth: the knowledge, reputation, contacts, imagination and commitment of the people who work for them.

It is self-evident, therefore, that one of the most important responsibilities of every employer, irrespective of size, is to put together and to nurture the best possible team of employees.

The task involves issues of workforce size, skill, morale, loyalty and productivity. It means addressing a long list of decisions, some everyday and immediate, some longer-term and gradual, about how to manage people – decisions about:

- appointments, pay negotiations and discipline;
- changes in the size of the labour force, and about which jobs should be done by that labour force and which subcontracted;
- developing and updating skills and changes in the demand for and supply of skills;
- how to get the best from people at work and how best to listen to their opinions, advice and concerns;
- how to lead them and give them a sense of pride in the organisation for which they work.

Organisations differ in how they tackle this responsibility – in how far it is seen as the collective responsibility of the most senior managers and how the responsibility is shared between line management and the personnel or human resources function.

Whichever balance is struck, the real challenge is to go beyond what is needed just to keep the system 'ticking over', to do more than just keep up with each day's demands and crises, and to know that you are making real, steady progress in building the very best possible human contribution to the success of your business.

In the process, there are three particular dangers. The first of these is simply that everyday, short-term pressures will swamp good planning and preparation, that reaction will replace strategy, and that decisions about people will be dominated by crisis and compulsion.

The second danger arises when, as so often, businesses are required to respond simultaneously to three imperatives:

- intense pressures for cost reduction;
- the need to keep customers loyal and happy with high-quality goods and services;
- the need to ensure that the employees in the business are content and productive.

Though these three imperatives are potentially in conflict, they can and should be kept in balance. In the real world, particularly when the pressures for cost reduction start to bite hard, it becomes intensely difficult to do this. A few companies have succeeded but in many cases at least one of the three requirements has suffered.

All too often, it is the well-being of the workforce that is neglected. While cost reductions are achieved through some form of redundancy or early retirement, other cuts may be made which take away the essential supports that people need to do their job well. Sensible economy turns into pressure, frustration and stress. There is a grave risk of a vicious circle, not immediately obvious to shareholders and customers, in which insecurity, fear and low morale combine with inadequate resources, and a heavy price is paid in long-term damage to the company and its reputation.

The third danger is that organisations faced with all these every-day pressures will fail to recognise where they are in the process of change. Businesses, like people, need to engage in a constant process of self-assessment in order to ensure that they know where they are and how to make the most of the stages that lie ahead. At what stage of development are we? Going round in circles, standing still – or using the experience of what has gone before as a platform from which to move forward?

Successful organisations must have the leadership and the humility to recognise the importance of such self-assessment. And in the process they need help and they need to listen.

Some of their most valuable helpers and sources of advice will be people who are themselves at a turning point in their lives and who also need support and understanding in their own transitions. The wise organisation is the one that manages both to hear the voice of experience and to give its older workers the support they need.

These are opportunities as well as dangers. The other side of the coin is that successful avoidance of these three dangers – continuing to plan ahead, keeping the balance between costs, customers and people and knowing where you have got to on the road ahead – is the hallmark of the successful organisation.

Our subject – the relationship between employment and age – is one important aspect of avoiding these dangers. Neglecting this subject can cause grave damage – and, as we shall see, has often done so. There are particular reasons, which will emerge in these pages, why issues of age profiles and balances and of the role of the older worker are dangerously neglected in the face of customer and cost reduction demands. If the future worth of a business is to be measured largely in terms of the knowledge and experience of its employees, what are we to make of policies and actions which seem designed to squander those very qualities?

We offer a counter to some of these dangers. Our aim is to show how it is possible to address the issues of employment and age while serving the wider interests of the business.

■ Why do older workers matter?

Before we examine the issues involved in more detail, it is worth listing briefly the business reasons why employers need an older element in their workforces. The reasons fall under six broad headings:[1]

Return on investment Employees who are older, and thus more likely to have had significant service with an employer, represent a heavy investment in training and a wealth of accumulated experience, which it is expensive to waste.

Response to skill shortages Older people are a source of skill and labour on which employers may come to depend when they can no longer rely on more traditional sources.

Maximising recruitment potential If older people are excluded from consideration for recruitment and promotion, the employer is likely to be ignoring a large proportion of the available talent and missing opportunities to acquire the best people with the necessary skills.

Response to demographic change Employers will increasingly need to take account of the ageing of the population both for recruitment purposes and in order to reflect the age profile of their customers.

Promoting diversity Older workers are a vital part of the mix in a well-balanced workforce – the 'memory' of the business, with whose help organisations make sure that they do not ignore the lessons of experience, and a steadying influence when morale is volatile and threatened.

Reputation Most employers will want to be regarded by present, future and indeed past employees as 'good employers' – with the reputation of looking after employees' needs at all stages of their careers.

If, on the other hand, older workers are neglected or effectively eliminated from the workforce, their employers run very serious risks:

- The investment in their training and their accumulated experience are wasted.

- The employer loses the ability to attract and retain older workers and recruitment choices become more limited.

- Projects and tasks are started from scratch, with insufficient account of experience; previous mistakes are ignored and precious time is wasted.

- Organisations develop a contagious atmosphere in which too many people are just waiting for the date of their early retirement – feeling insecure and apprehensive and therefore less productive, instead of making a positive contribution to a well-motivated workforce.

- The organisation loses the reputation of looking after all its employees throughout their working lives and addressing the special needs of new recruits, of those with families or caring responsibilities, of women, and of employees approaching retirement.

- False assumptions about the capacity and contribution of older employees become self-fulfilling, so that the damage caused by their neglect is reinforced and multiplied.

Any of these risks can hurt an organisation. When they come together, as they so often do through neglect and 'short-termism', they can do serious damage.

▪ The changing face of employment

Before we can draw any conclusions about how to make the most constructive use of older workers, we need to examine in more detail some very important changes and trends in patterns of employment which are now occurring, their causes and their relevance to older workers.

Future observers are likely to look back on the mid-1990s not only as a pivotal time in the economic cycle but as a turning point in many aspects of employment: its quality and risks, the different forms it takes, how it is distributed, the impact of demographic change, and the effect on employment of economic recession.

Not all the changes which we are now experiencing will be looked back upon as beneficial. Mark Twain quipped that 'if work were so great, the rich would have hogged it long ago'. Charles Handy comments that indeed they have. The result, he says, is that some have work and money and too little time, while others have all the time but no work and no money.[2]

In the remainder of this chapter, we look at six different ways in which the current labour market is developing, each with particular implications for older workers. The list does not include the specific issues which are addressed more fully in later chapters, such as workforce reduction and equal opportunities. It does, however, represent a combination of major changes in our working environment and culture which employers need to recognise and turn to their advantage. We suggest ways in which they can do so.

▪ The demographic factors

It was in 1995 that we were to have seen the explosion of the 'demographic time bomb'. The phrase was not created by scaremongers; it was used in the title of a report published by the National Economic Development Office.[3] This was going to be the year in which the low UK birth rate of the 1970s would mean that employers and universities faced drastic declines in the availability of young people.

There was real concern at the time. It was reported that half of all the girls leaving school with the necessary qualifications would be needed simply to meet the need of the National Health Service for nurses. Employers were urged to turn their recruitment activities to less familiar sources – including older people, the unemployed and people with disabilities – to make up for the expected shortage of young men and women.

But, as a recent article put it, 'this threatened crisis, which captured the minds of economists, politicians and the public, never happened. The decline in numbers was inevitable but it has not precipitated the labour shortages and empty lecture halls predicted at the end of the last decade.'[4]

This is partly because new groups of employees, particularly women, have entered the labour market in sufficient numbers to compensate for the shortage of young people. Above all, the demographic factors have been masked by recession. An employer who has been reducing numbers by putting a total freeze on recruitment is not likely to be familiar with the state of the external labour market and the shortages that it may contain, either today or in the relatively near future. The less skilled jobs, which were seen as more suitable for younger employees, are not now needed in anything like the same numbers, as technology and cost pressures exert their own effects on the nature and content of work.

A useful measure of the situation is seen in graduate recruitment. Newly qualified graduates still find that it is not they but employers who are in the buyers' market. Unemployment among graduates is still high, at 10.5 per cent, though dropping. Students and parents, who once thought that the 1990s would bring real relief to their fears of continued high levels of youth unemployment, are asking what the economists of the time were talking about.

But if the explosion of the time bomb has been prevented by recession, employers need to remember that recessions, however long drawn out, are temporary – whereas the demographic factors are permanent and inevitable.

The combination of increased life expectancy, changes in birth rates (particularly the large numbers born between the late 1950s and early 1970s) and the movement of the 'cohorts' or generations involved through their working lives and into retirement means that:

- The number of people under 16 dropped by 2.6 million (22 per cent) between 1971 and 1991.

- The number of people aged 16–29 will have dropped by the end of the century from 12.3 million in 1991 to 10.2 million in 2001 (21 per cent).

- The number of people aged 50–64 will have increased from 8.9 million in 1991 to 10.2 million in 2001 (15 per cent) and by a further 2.1 million by 2021 (21 per cent).[5]

Put in another way:

- In 1971, one in four people in the population was under 24, one in ten was between 65 and 79, and one in 43 was over 80.

- In 2050, only one in six will be under 24, one in seven will be between 65 and 79, and one in ten will be over 80.

Population changes 1971–2050

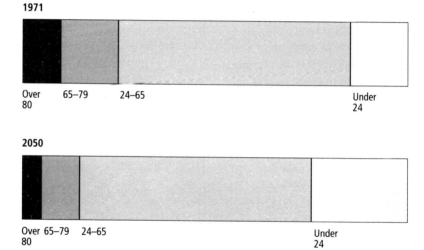

1971

Over 80   65–79   24–65   Under 24

2050

Over 80 65–79   24–65   Under 24

In short, as our population grows older because of better health care and as the number of young people declines because of the effect of declining birth rates, employers will have to look very carefully to the future to assess what their labour requirements will be and what likelihood there is of their being able to meet them in the light of these projections.

There are also going to be major changes not just in the profile of the population but also in the shape of the workforce.

- In 1986, 23 per cent of the workforce was under 24 and 31 per cent was over 45.

- In 1996, only 15 per cent will be under 24 while 33 per cent will be over 45.

- By 2006, 37 per cent will be over 45.[6]

At present, average ages within companies are tending to fall as workforce reductions based on early retirement remove large proportions of older workers. But employers should not have to learn the hard way that, as the population ages, they are going to have to adapt their own workforces accordingly.

It is no good employers just noticing in passing that the demographic time bomb did not go off. If they have not yet worked out the implications of the demographic changes for their employment requirements in the medium and long term, they have only themselves to blame – and cause for blame there will certainly be.

The recession has meant that many employers have become unfamiliar with recruiting. If those employers expect an upturn in consumer demand by the end of the decade or before, and if they assume that the labour market is likely to look much the same by then as it does today, they are going to have to do a lot of explaining to shareholders if market opportunities are missed – and if others who have taken account of the demographic factors have taken action.

A little work now on skill and number requirements at intervals over the next five years, and on the consequences for policies on recruitment, training, retirement and redundancy, could save some painful awakenings in the period ahead.

Personnel planning has become too closely equated with simple cost reduction. A company which has failed to provide the resources to compete is just as badly placed as one which has grown too fat.

- Recruitment of older workers

In the very limited recruitment that has been taking place in the 1990s, the share represented by older workers has been disproportionately low. This is partly because of direct and indirect discrimination and partly because employers have seen an inconsistency between any recruitment of older workers and earlier workforce reductions based largely on early retirement.

But the employment scene is changing fast. The gradual process of emergence from recession will require employers to anticipate and address unfamiliar issues of skill shortage and competition for labour. Traditional supplies of skill may become insufficient and they will need to look at less familiar sources, including older people, as potential recruits.

Systems of recruitment will need to be reviewed to make sure that they can reach out to these new sources. Even though this sort of recruitment requirement may not be immediate, employers who fail to plan in advance may find their competitors getting there first.

Many organisations' recruitment systems have tended to concentrate on the engagement of young people and to build their processes around their particular needs and attributes. They are in danger of missing perfectly acceptable candidates from other age groups. Younger recruiters may also tend to recruit in their own image, with the same risk.

Employers need to think about the long-term composition of their workforce and particularly to make sure that they have the right balance of skill and experience; that they know what is happening to the age profile and average age of their workforce, and why and how they wish to influence both.

During the 1980s, the age profiles of organisations were distorted by two parallel processes. Freezes on the recruitment of young people combined with workforce reductions targeted on older workers, and the result was a sharp increase in the proportion of employees in their 30s and 40s and an accompanying decline in the numbers of younger and older workers. Unless checked, these trends will produce serious distortions in labour supply and availability in the decades ahead.

It is too easy to forget the importance of retaining and valuing within the workforce a sufficient proportion of employees with long-term knowledge and experience of the business and of the influences which have shaped it; people with the ability to deploy that knowledge both in everyday operations and in longer-term planning. As one manager (from Unigate) put it:

'There is a tremendous value associated with long service, with people who have grown up with a business, who understand what it was and what it has become, who know the short cuts to getting things done, how to cut through bureaucracy to get a result, who understand at a fundamental level the complexities of the business they're in because of their experience and knowledge gained over many years.'

The process of matching supply and demand, anticipating changes in both, and doing something about it in advance is a central, critical task in any business. It is most familiar in products and services – having the right product available in the right quantity at the time and place in which customers want it. Too many businesses know the price of failure in any part of this jigsaw – of failing to start on the research and development planning required to bring the right product to the market on time, of failing to know what competitors are up to and of failing to find out what the market wants.

Exactly the same issues apply to the supply and demand for labour. What types of skills do we want? When, where and in what quantity? How easily are we going to be able to find them? The difference is that employers tend to pay far less attention to looking at labour requirements in this way than they do to looking at product requirements. Labour may not be seen as such a priority now – but the cost of failure is just as great.

The reasons for this apparent neglect are complex. They include the long-running debate about the place of human resources issues in employers' priorities, the tendency to regard recruitment as a separate, specialist science best left to experts, or not as a science at all but as a task which will take care of itself. How many company conferences or board meetings regularly include items about the people in the business on the agenda?

This neglect may have been reinforced by recession. When they have taken place, discussions about people have tended to be dominated by plans for getting rid of them. The term 'manpower planning' has become unfamiliar (and not just because of its apparently sexist implications).

It is no less important for a business to look at its labour requirements when it is at the bottom of an economic cycle than when it is prospering. The combination of economic recovery and the decline in the number of school leavers means that businesses could be facing real skill shortages by the end of the decade. Indeed, in a recent study of over 400 firms, one in two said that they thought that their profitability would be affected over the next 12 months as a consequence of not having young people with suitable skills.[7]

This has already been recognised by a number of employers, notably in the retail industry,[8] who have chosen to concentrate their recruitment in certain locations on older workers. Their reasons have included:

- concerns about future shortages of competent school leavers, on whom they have traditionally relied for recruitment;

- their ability to train older workers relatively swiftly;

- the greater willingness of older workers to fit in with the flexible working patterns, often on a part-time basis, required by retailers to cover evenings and weekends;

- the cost-effectiveness of part-time working;

- the desire to match the age profile of their employees with that of their customers.

W H Smith, commenting on this last objective, refer to their awareness that shopping is an increasingly important means of socialising for older customers:

> 'Many may prefer to be served by someone of their own age, and we are sensitive to the fact that a preponderance of younger employees may inhibit older customers from shopping with us. For us, it is about having a balance; having a diverse workforce which matches more closely our diverse customer base.'[9]

Employers who for whatever reason wish to recruit in this way will also need to consider the particular requirements of older employees for:

- full integration into the workforce;

- reintroduction to the working environment, for those who have not worked for some time;

- induction into an unfamiliar organisation;

- updating of out-of-date skills, particularly in information technology (our discussions confirmed widespread fears on the part of older workers about the mysteries of IT, alongside remarkable acceptance and dexterity once the initial barriers and unfamiliarity had been overcome);

- flexible systems of training which suit older people's capacity for learning (in particular their preference for learning on the job rather than by classroom/textbook methods);

- good, ergonomically designed work stations (which older people need, but from which all will benefit).

The case study below describes the pioneering initiatives taken by B&Q at two of their locations to recruit only employees aged over 50 and the important lessons they drew from them.

B&Q A store completely staffed by older workers

B&Q is the country's largest home improvement retailer. Founded in 1969, the company now has 280 'Supercentre' and Warehouse stores around the UK.

At the end of the 1980s, B&Q recognised that the demographic situation was changing. With fewer younger workers entering the labour market, there needed to be a radical review of future employment plans. In the biggest DIY business and with customers ranging from 'the trade' to DIY enthusiasts, B&Q had already recognised the benefits that more mature and experienced employees could deliver.

This combination of track record and changing labour market encouraged B&Q to pilot a store in Macclesfield which would be completely staffed with people over the age of 50, to show that the over-50s could do all the jobs necessary to run a successful DIY store.

As described below, the experiment was a great success. It was repeated in a new store opened in 1990 in Exmouth in Devon.

At Macclesfield, B&Q decided that it would need to extend the usual period of preparation and training before the opening of the store to provide special training for the older employees. This would include training in information technology – essential for operating a store.

In the event, the extra time proved unnecessary; indeed the older employees brought with them a wide range of skills and experience. The Exmouth store subsequently opened within the normal timescale.

The experience of both these stores has had a very positive effect on attitudes throughout the company, and store managers who saw the results began actively to encourage older people to apply for jobs in their own stores. The value of the older worker is now positively recognised throughout the company and reflected in its recruiting literature and practice.

The experiments were a dramatic way of showing people in the company and elsewhere that older employees have a major contribution to make. Neither store now feels that it is necessary to restrict recruitment to the over-50s, as B&Q believes that a broad mixture of ages has most to offer to its customers, but the message which the experiments conveyed has been of great value.

The specific benefits which B&Q now reports from having a good mix of employees of all ages include:

- a highly effective sharing of diverse experiences in training programmes (in which the older employees are rapidly able to overcome fears about working in a new environment and to polish their communication skills);

- the availability of excellent role models for younger employees;

- the presence in the workforce of people who are likely to be home owners and therefore to have a real interest in and knowledge of DIY;

- the ability to pass on that knowledge to younger employees within the working environment;

- the welcome by customers of staff of their own generation who talk the same language and who are able and willing to spend time with them discussing their requirements and helping them with their queries;

- the addition to the workforce of people who may have done relevant jobs elsewhere – for example plumbing, building and electrical work;

- a positive change in management attitudes towards older staff;

- the development of a more caring and consultative management style;

- a valuable source of information and ideas to management – for example on health and safety and opportunities for cutting costs;

- a willingness to accept more flexible patterns of working – for example weekend or evening shifts, which may be less suitable for younger employees with more family ties.

B&Q does not enforce retirement. Both new and existing employees above the normal retirement age of 60 may be given the opportunity to continue to work on a fixed-term contract. B&Q's oldest current employee is 82.

One bank, not one of our participants, spoke of the 'baby bankers' issue, referring to concern on the part of older corporate clients about the steady and continuing reduction in the age of the bank representatives with whom they are being asked to deal. The same organisation – which, unlike some, was fully aware of the average age of its workforce, 32 – also spoke of the concern felt by people over that age that they might be regarded as 'over the hill', even though many of them were in reality at the peak of their career in their 40s.

The idea of seeking specific benefits from the employment of older workers is more familiar in the United States than in the UK. Examples include First American Bank, which uses highly educated retirees as on-call tellers; American Airlines, which has trained over 300 older workers in the 40–65 bracket as flight attendants to raise its appeal to older clients; Betz Laboratories of Pennsylvania, which has hired older workers to reduce staff turnover, and Texas Refinery Corporation, nearly 500 of whose sales force of 3,000 are in their 60s, 70s and 80s and are found to relate better to senior citizen property owners.[10]

A group of health centres in Florida providing non-acute services to older patients is staffed by retired doctors, who are delighted to give their services free of charge one day a week to 'keep their hand in', and to provide advice, counselling and routine medical care to patients who warmly appreciate the services of professionals of their own age.

In response to the changes described earlier in this chapter, several exciting and innovative projects are springing up to provide practical help and the chance of a new economic role for older people who are out of work. All of them need, and are starting to receive, support from employers as part of the business contribution to help tackle unemployment and support older people in their search for new opportunities.

One of the most remarkable of these is POPE, which is described in a case study at the end of this chapter. Another is the Third Age Network in Guildford, with offshoots in other locations in south-east England, which has been working away steadily over the last two years in finding new opportunities, mainly for redundant professional people. A further example is the Mature Workers' Register in Bournemouth, an area of 19 per cent unemployment. Under this scheme, some 200 people from all walks of life have been trained; 50 have been placed in full-time jobs and many others in part-time work, self-employment or further training, at a cost of only £500 per job filled. Other projects have recently started in Wrexham, York, north Nottinghamshire, Falkirk, the Isle of Arran, Bristol and Brent (London).

These projects come together in a project called the Third Age Challenge Trust, which provides a forum for sharing good practice between projects and gives practical help in setting them up.

When recruiting, companies may forget the services of the Jobcentres. They are well worth using, not least to ensure access to the widest possible sources of recruitment – and not just for less senior jobs. As we shall see, the Jobcentres have taken a positive approach to finding work for older people, and employers who maintain regular contact with them are helping the Employment Service in its vital task of helping to find work for unemployed people.

▪ Core workers and subcontractors

For older workers and their employers, the growth of subcontracting poses both threats and opportunities. The main threats are that it will reduce the amount of permanent employment, that this reduction will be at the expense of older workers, and that knowledge and experience of the business will be sacrificed for the more obvious advantages of subcontracting. On the other hand, this type of employment, which can often be arranged on a part-time and flexible basis, may be particularly well suited to older workers. There are also interesting opportunities, which are illustrated by the case studies on Skillbase and the Travelers Corporation in Chapter 6, for using former employees themselves as subcontractors.

Employers have found increasing merit in having a variety of tasks undertaken by subcontractors rather than by the permanent, core workforce. This trend, whose spread has been anticipated by Charles Handy and other observers,[11] is now a strong feature of the UK labour market. But the practice, and its potential for abuse, has a long history

– for example in subcontract design in the engineering industry and in 'lump' labour in the building industry.

Thirty-eight per cent of all UK workers (9.7 million) are in what has been described as the flexible workforce: temporary workers, the self-employed, part-timers. This type of work has always been more prevalent among women – who represent 50 per cent of the flexible workforce – but the proportion of men within it has started to grow more recently.[12]

The most familiar motive for an employer subcontracting work has been the ability to accommodate peaks and troughs of labour demand, whether caused by fluctuations in customer requirements or seasonal variations. It also gives the employer access to a wider base of skills without having to retain them permanently. And of course peripheral workers do not need permanent office space and the overheads that go with it.

Many employers who have decided to subcontract substantial parts of their work have done so in order to concentrate their permanent employment on skills which are peculiar to their business: skills which are available on the general labour market they regard as capable of being purchased from outside as required. 'Our task is to be expert in banking/oil extraction/telecoms, etc not in catering/security/ transport, etc.' This type of subcontracting is most familiar in technical and ancillary functions, such as catering and security, but it is also starting to happen at more senior levels – with parts of functions such as accountancy and personnel being subcontracted.

A further aspect has been the development of businesses which themselves specialise in the provision of subcontract labour, ranging from the familiar temporary secretarial agencies through to the large-scale, multi-skill providers such as Manpower.

Employers using temporary or subcontract labour in this way need also to be aware of the potential disadvantages. In theory, the productivity of temporary employees may be lower than that of permanent staff because of their lack of permanent identification with the business. Because they have no prospect of promotion or advancement, they may lack motivation. In practice, this will depend very much on the care with which the supplier of temporary staff selects, trains and employs them.

Manpower plc Employment of temporary staff

Over many years, Manpower has developed a relationship with the staff whom it supplies which goes far beyond the intermediary role which many associate with providers of temporary staff. The staff all have contracts of employment which guarantee their employment rights and benefits and also provide ample opportunity for training and skill enhancement. In this way, Manpower is able to provide the flexibility which is the essence of its service while still protecting the security of the employee. Given the security which staff enjoy and the real possibility of career progression within Manpower, the productivity of the staff it supplies is in almost every case just as high as that of its counterparts who are directly employed by its clients.

Unless this sort of approach is taken towards the provision of temporary employees, there is a danger that a form of 'class distinction' may emerge in employment, with a sharp divide between the relatively secure, permanent, pensioned, full-time core worker on the one hand and the part-time, insecure, non-pensioned, subcontract worker on the other.

The danger is illustrated in the development of so-called zero hours contracts under which individuals are contracted to work at hourly rates for whatever number and combination of hours the employer decides, ranging from zero to 40 or more per week, often at short notice and sometimes including onerous restrictions on (or even exclusion of) work for other employers.

In his assessment of where the nation stands at the end of the 1990s, Will Hutton paints a stark picture of who's who in employment: 'Only around 40 per cent of the workforce enjoy tenured full-time employment or secure self-employment . . .; another 30 per cent are insecurely self-employed, involuntarily part-time, or casual workers; while the bottom 30 per cent, the marginalised, are idle or working for poverty wages.'[13]

For both employers and providers of subcontract labour, the undoubted benefits of subcontracting need to be accompanied by policies which

- reduce the risks of exploitation and abuse;

- recognise the limitations of subcontract staff, and do not make unreasonable demands on them;

- promote good employment standards within subcontract agencies and suppliers;
- develop the concept of subcontract labour as a respected and attractive alternative form of employment.

■ No more 'jobs for life'

Until the 1960s, there were widespread areas of employment in which people could expect to spend their entire careers, from traditional apprenticeship through to retirement. Many organisations had a tradition of high security of employment. As a result, their workforces would typically have had an evenly spread age profile, with a strong presence of older employees, and the experience and wisdom that goes with them.

Employment which can be regarded as 'safe' or permanent has now virtually disappeared. The 1960s and 1970s saw a sharp decline in manufacturing industry, involving widespread redundancy programmes, both voluntary and compulsory, in the private sector. The 1980s and 1990s have seen the same relative insecurity of employment spread to sectors previously regarded as providing relatively permanent employment – central and local government, the now privatised utilities, the armed services, health and education, and those few private sector companies which could once offer such comfort. (We discuss in Chapter 5 how widely this more recent trend has been based on voluntary early retirement, whether voluntary is really voluntary and how long such voluntarism is likely to last.)

Organisations which have hitherto placed a strong emphasis on job security are now seeing a greater likelihood of shorter stays by employees, a greater willingness to recruit externally where necessary and a growth in subcontracting.

On the other hand, although these have been significant trends in the UK, they have been even sharper elsewhere in Europe, where the share of temporary employment is generally higher than ours.

Perceptions of careers by employers and employed are changing fast:

- Diversity of experience within an organisation is now valued as highly as a vertical climb within a specialism.
- There is less opportunity for vertical careers as organisations become flatter.
- Experience gained with several different employers is seen as an asset on a CV.
- Loyalty and commitment are no longer being expressed and measured in terms of long service.
- There is a growing acceptance of 'horizontal' career development.

These developments, together with the increase in subcontracting, mark the end of an era in which both employers and employees could plan for lifetime employment in one place. Future employment patterns will be far more flexible and varied, calling in turn for much greater self-sufficiency on the part of employees in planning their own careers, including the acquisition and updating of skills (to which we return in Chapter 3).

A British trade union leader[14] recently quoted the following figures on the average number of years for which individuals stay with one employer:

Japan	**9.0**	France	**4.8**
USA	**8.7**	UK	**2.2**
Germany	**5.5**		

Charles Handy has forecast a new concept in the adaptation of working lives, coining the expression 'portfolio careers'. He welcomes the news that, as organisations reshape themselves, we will all be 'portfolio people' – increasingly dividing our lives between different forms of paid work, whether through wages (earned inside the organisation) or fees (earned outside it), and unpaid or 'free' work, which might be looking after the home and family, voluntary work done outside the home for charities, neighbours or the community, or studying.[15]

Views may differ as to how many of us will alter our lives to that extent but, as individuals change their expectations of work and their attitudes towards it, employers need to think carefully about the type of employment which they themselves want to offer – and what repu-tation they want to have in the recruitment market. Clearly prepara-tion of this sort on the part of employers will benefit not only the recruitment process but also policies and practices for those already in employment whom employers need to retain.

If employers conclude, as many have, that they are no longer able to sell themselves to present and future employees as providing permanent, secure, long-term employment, they need to present the alternatives in a positive way and to consider employee needs at the various stages of their individual working lives – even if it is not to be for the whole of those working lives.

The elements of a positive, alternative pattern of working include:

- induction training;

- explaining and projecting the career opportunities which do exist;

- providing access to employment at all ages instead of concentrating only on young people and long-term career development;

- providing and updating skills;

- appraisal and development of employees;

- efficient and comfortable working environments;

- well planned and supported transitions towards redundancy and retirement.

All this gives rise to several age-related issues. Employers need to remember that the trend towards shorter careers makes it much harder to accumulate experience and knowledge of their business and that, in a labour market which is more volatile and fast-moving, it may be less easy to retain much-needed skill and experience. Most importantly, employers will need to adapt their employment and recruitment practices to enable them to take on people at all stages of their working lives and to move away from the tradition of concen-trating recruitment on young people with the prospect of long, verti-cal careers in the same business.

These changes will put a high premium on supporting employees and meeting their needs at the different stages of their working lives and making sure that they are enabled to update their skills and keep up with the process of learning not just when they arrive but through-out their period of employment.

▪ New organisations and structures

Alongside reductions in the size of organisations, there have been widespread changes in their structure and shape – for all sorts of rea-sons. These have a particular relevance to older employees because of their ability to bring their experience to bear on the process of change.

Some organisations, for example in local government and the health service, have had reorganisation imposed on them from out-side. Some have decided on a shift of authority from the centre to the parts; some have done exactly the opposite. (And some have actually done both in the space of a few years!) Some have reorganised in order to match the 'segmentation' of their customers. Others have based new structures on the classification of their products.

Some, for example in the newly privatised industries, have found it necessary to engineer wholesale changes of culture. Others have undertaken far-reaching programmes of change, self-examination and reform under the headings of total quality management, matrix man-agement, re-engineering or whatever new banners are offered by the business schools and consultants, often involving newly discovered statements of corporate values and organisational mission.

Much of this work has been a force for good, for much-needed reform, greater clarity of purpose, efficiency and better service to cus-tomers – and it would be cynical and unfair to dismiss it. However, the other side of the coin is the disruption and instability which can accompany constant processes of reorganisation, as employers strug-gle to come to terms with the inevitability of some form of federalism.

Our discussions revealed that many managers and others recog-nised the benefits of such reforms but longed for periods of stability in which to capitalise upon them, often struggling to produce the results required of them under the twin pressures of reduced resources and constant organisational change. In a series of regional conferences held in 1994 and 1995 as part of the Carnegie Third Age Programme, it was remarkable how many participants singled out this particular concern as a barrier to effective working.

These comments, which were especially marked in the local government sector, were not generally made in an atmosphere of opposition to inevitable change. Rather, they were genuine concerns and frustrations on the part of otherwise positive individuals that their organisations had been diverted from their true purpose by a process of restructuring that was so continuous and time-consuming that it was not only difficult to work effectively within these organisations but also very hard to engage satisfactorily with them from outside. Of particular concern is the way in which reorganisation can freeze and delay important developments and projects. 'We can't really start that until this new structure has settled down.'

None of this is to argue against reorganisation. Indeed, it is inevitable that dynamic and successful businesses will be involved in virtually constant restructuring of one sort or another. The organisation which neither adapts to changes in the outside world nor generates self-improvement from within is unlikely to prosper or even survive.

However, our discussions suggest strongly that the process of change is far more likely to be a force for good if those planning it remember three simple maxims which are particularly relevant to the older employee.

Learn from previous reorganisations

Restructuring exercises are too often dominated by considerations of 'not invented here', by a desire for change for its own sake rather than to achieve a specific improvement. Older employees have an important role in bringing earlier experience to bear on the process of change and in helping to avoid earlier mistakes.

Listen before deciding

We saw a direct correlation between successful change and the distance from the workplace at which it was decided. The least successful changes were those imposed from outside, followed by those decided behind closed doors by small groups of very senior managers. At the other end of the scale came the most valuable reforms – generated from within and initiated by constantly listening to employee opinions and concerns.

This does not imply any abandonment of decision-making and leadership but the simple, time-worn truth that decisions are likely to be better and more easily implemented if they are taken after listening to those who will be most affected by them.

Good organisations are about good relationships

I remember a discussion at board level in one organisation about the qualities which should be aimed for and developed in managers. I had been asked to produce my own list in order of priority as a basis for discussion. The quality I put at the top was courtesy (followed by courage) – which provoked an explosion of disagreement from some round the table. I still believe it comes top: management through trust and respect and not by frightening or bullying people. As Tom Peters put it: 'Relationships really are all there is.'[16]

Simple and obvious as this advice may be, our discussions suggested that an alarming number of large organisations are today operating under par because of fears about workforce reduction combined with excessive or mishandled reorganisation.

In all these processes, the voice, advice and opinions of the older generation of employees can make all the difference in bringing about necessary change in an informed and effective way. The alternative is serious damage to both morale and performance.

▪ Flexible working arrangements

Last in this list of changes comes the rapid development of much more flexible patterns of working for individuals. These are often well suited to older employees and so provide an important opportunity to retain and motivate them.

Every one of the organisations taking part in our study has extended the opportunities for flexible working in a great variety of ways, including:

- part-time working, for various purposes: for example for new parents, for carers, before retirement;
- flexitime;
- career breaks;
- sabbaticals;
- parental leave, including paternity leave and leave for family reasons;
- weekend and evening working;
- job-sharing;
- short-term contracts;
- zero hours contracts (working as and when required);
- teleworking/homeworking;
- annualised hours (in which the annual hours of an individual employee are varied in a defined period (daily, weekly, quarterly) within an agreed total for the year);
- gradual or phased retirement;
- term-time contracts.

These arrangements reflect the combined needs of employers and employees. Employers, facing growing competitive pressure, need better coverage of customer needs, fuller use of plant and equipment and new ways of reducing costs and increasing productivity. Employees face a whole range of demands on their working time – for example to accommodate partners with their own careers, to make time to pursue their education, to look after their children or dependent relatives.

These forms of flexible working may not always represent welcome and constructive choices for individual employees but they reflect the necessity to achieve the difficult balance between the demands of family life and the need for income. Sometimes flexible work patterns, for example on shifts, at weekends or in the evenings, may be the only form of work that is available.

The opportunities for employers, and the scope for innovation, are enormous – especially in avoiding the loss of skill and experience, and the subsequent recruitment and training costs involved in having to replace employees who cannot combine their personal lives with full-time work and who are lost to the employer for that reason alone.

A study for the Institute of Personnel Management (as it then was) suggested that flexible employees may often be more productive.[17] Part-time workers suffer less end-of-the-day fatigue and short-term employees may be better able to work under pressure, knowing that it is for a limited period. Flexible workers tend to have less absenteeism, perhaps because it is easier for part-time or shift employees to arrange visits to doctors and dentists outside working hours.

The Government has encouraged flexible working. The Department of Employment (now merged with the Department of Education) has, for example, produced a guide on teleworking offering examples of good practice and ways of overcoming potential disadvantages.[18]

As the pattern of work gradually changes from a full-time, five day a week basis towards a whole range of non-standard patterns, employers will increasingly need to consider how to ensure that flexible employees are still given the necessary opportunities for training, promotion and the maximum integration into the business.

It would be a missed opportunity as well as a waste of talent if the inevitable growth in flexible working were to produce a new form of industrial apartheid, with those working in non-standard ways either less privileged or viewed as less able to carry senior responsibility. What an excellent example it would be if we were to see a chief executive or a finance director operating a job-share. Perhaps there are some.

As things stand, it is far harder for part-timers to gain promotion, and part-time work in more senior positions is much more rarely found in the UK than elsewhere.[19]

Flexible patterns of work are often well suited to the needs and attributes of older employees. Parents whose children have left home may be far more willing to work unusual hours, for example at weekends and in the evening. It would be good to see the development of job-sharing between older and younger employees, with the transfer of skills combining with the more flexible hours involved so as to benefit both parties to the job-share and the employers – but only if the pension barriers which we discuss in the next chapter (see pp 51–53) can be overcome.

Employers can also use flexible patterns of work, such as home-working and teleworking, part-time working and career breaks, to respond to the caring and other domestic needs of older employees, thus enabling them to retain the valuable qualities of those older employees.

What is good for older employees is usually good for all

The experience of employers who have developed these employment and recruitment practices is that they have derived benefits for the whole of their workforce. They have also paid tribute to the resultant benefits in customer relations, labour turnover (which is actually lower among older employees than younger) and the less measurable but vitally important 'working atmosphere' – to which older workers have consistently contributed maturity, humour, sound advice and a wealth of personal expertise.

For some employers, the actions and precautions suggested in this chapter will be remedial measures – they may even be regarded as bolting the stable door after the horse has bolted. But if businesses have been damaged by neglect of these matters – and many have – they are no less important; it simply means that redressing the damage will take more time.

The POPE project Finding jobs for unemployed older people

In 1992, the Bradford and District Training and Enterprise Council (TEC) entered a proposal in the Government-sponsored 'TEC Challenge' competition, seeking funds for a Bradford-based scheme to assist unemployed individuals aged 50 or over into jobs. The project was called POPE – 'People of Previous Experience'.

The main elements of the POPE proposal were as follows:

- creation of a register of unemployed people aged 50 or over seeking work in the area;

- in parallel, identification of employers with suitable vacancies;

- a matching service between the two, free of charge to both individuals and employers;

- a subsidy of £2,000 payable to the employer concerned for each vacancy filled.

The job subsidy was to be paid only for newly created jobs filled by people of 50 or over who had been unemployed for at least 26 weeks at the time and if the placement eventually lasted for six months or more.

The proposal was accepted and the POPE scheme was duly launched in October 1993. It remains in successful operation.

By the end of its first year it had achieved most but not all of its targets. It had made 110 placements (target 120), of which:

- 80 were from among the long-term unemployed (target 50);

- 81 were placed in newly created jobs (target 90);

- 89 (81 per cent) were still in employment after six months.

Subsidies were paid for 64 of these placements which met all three criteria.

A surprising but quite consistent result is that it has been virtually impossible to involve large firms in POPE, although there are several in Bradford, including some major company headquarters. The reasons are not entirely clear: many have been involved in heavy redundancy programmes; most said that they were not recruiting.

Small firms thus represent the vast bulk of the employers who have registered vacancies. POPE's observation is that it is

even more important for them than for larger firms to get each appointment right first time, especially as they have much less opportunity than employers with a sizeable workforce to adjust unsuitable appointments. Accordingly the smaller firms were keen to consider a wide range of candidates and placed greater value on the experience and reliability of older candidates.

The vast majority of vacancies registered initially were one-off vacancies for individuals, although several of the firms came back to POPE as repeat customers and continue to do so. It was found that, in order to satisfy employers' needs, POPE needed to have a wide variety of candidates on the register.

POPE employs a staff of five, all of whom have experience of being unemployed themselves; it was initially based in the TEC offices in Bradford. It works with the advice of a steering group involving managers of local Jobcentres, employers, people involved in education, Bradford City Council and other individuals.

There has been enormous interest in the POPE project. Its staff confirm that quite a large proportion of their time is spent telling other people about the scheme. They have no complaint about this, however: they are keen to tell the story and very much hope that the scheme will be emulated by others.

POPE has an exciting future. By virtually all its measures it has been an outstanding success, reflecting great credit on Bradford and District TEC. Few other TECs or LECs seem to have made this degree of commitment to older people and the results speak for themselves.

The TEC is now entering the next, developmental phase of POPE's work in a new partnership with the W H Morrison Trust, a charitable foundation established by a local employer, with additional mainstream funding from the European Social Fund (Objective 3). Both the TEC and the Trust are active partners in the running of POPE, and the funding is secure for the next two years at least.

Some of the features of the scheme have been changed for the second phase of operation. The age limit has been dropped from 50 to 40. This is partly because POPE's experience is that age discrimination is not limited to those over 50 and partly because it will extend the opportunities provided by the scheme to a larger group of applicants.

From 1995 onwards, there were no new subsidies payable to employers. The subsidy played a useful purpose in the first stage: although the payment was relatively small, it succeeded in attracting the necessary initial interest. POPE's view, now being confirmed, is that the scheme is quite viable without the subsidy.

The most important change, however, building on the experience of the first year, is starting to develop POPE into a new and enhanced service for older people.

POPE found that many job applicants who had been unemployed for more than a few months were ill equipped for the task of seeking new employment. They were worn down by the constant experience of rejection by employers. Their skills were out of date. They lacked the paperwork, such as a CV, which would form the basis of employers' decisions as to whether to put them on to shortlists; information about themselves was often limited to the brief material which POPE had obtained about them in an initial interview and their own, usually handwritten, material. Many were totally unfamiliar with job interviews; one 63-year-old had not been interviewed since he was 14. Some were totally resigned to being unemployed after 50.

These conclusions will come as no surprise to those used to working with the long-term unemployed but their confirmation in Bradford persuaded POPE to offer its registered applicants, from 1995 onwards, a one-week programme of training and counselling – free of charge and using the most up-to-date counselling techniques, in which all the POPE staff have been trained.

This is a massive enhancement of the counselling provided in the first year of the scheme, which was limited to about one hour and devoted almost exclusively to finding out enough about applicants to help match them with vacancies.

The new programme is aimed at helping individual applicants to help themselves by

- analysing their skills;
- improving their job search skills;
- helping them produce high-quality CVs;
- preparing them for interviews;

- helping them develop individual goals and plans;

- assisting them with access to necessary training;

- building their motivation and confidence.

In the second year of operation, still better results were being achieved. By November 1995, 133 more people had been assisted into jobs (target 100), 8,667 hours of guidance and counselling had been given (target 10,780) and 271 people had joined the guidance programme (target 368). Looking further ahead, Bradford TEC, in partnership with other European organisations, had obtained approval in principle for support from the EU 'HORIZON' Fund for a major expansion of the POPE project on a unified, transitional basis.

Employers' action points

DEMOGRAPHIC FACTORS

- Do you know what current and future demographic trends mean for your business – for example for the supply of school leavers and graduates?

- Have you thought about how the ageing of the population will affect your organisation, your customers and your workforce?

RECRUITMENT

- Have you anticipated the skills and numbers of employees you will require in one, five and ten years' time?

- Will you be able to compete for labour with other employers?

- Are your recruitment systems and staff geared to recruiting from unfamiliar sources, including older workers? Or do they concentrate too much on younger workers?

- Have you got the right balance of skill, experience and long-term knowledge of your organisation?

CORE AND SUBCONTRACT EMPLOYMENT

- Do you have a policy about which jobs should be done by your own staff and which should be subcontracted?

- If so – or if you are preparing one – what is the purpose of the policy:

To help deal with peaks and troughs of demand?
To widen the range of staff available to you?
To cut down on overheads?
To limit your permanent employment to the skills which are peculiar to your business?

- Do you have standards of employment which you require from agencies providing you with temporary staff?

SECURITY OF EMPLOYMENT AND CAREER PATTERNS

- Do you want current and potential employees to think of themselves as having a career with your organisation?
- What value do you place on long service? How do you recognise and reward it?
- What help do you provide in helping employees to plan their careers?

FLEXIBLE WORKING

- What forms of flexible working do you provide?
- What are the objectives of your flexible work arrangements:
  To provide a better service to customers?
  To reduce costs?
  To make better use of equipment?
  To help to meet the needs of employees in matching their personal and working lives?

3 The needs of older workers

If employers are to realise the potential of older employees, they must understand their needs. In this chapter, we look at five different sets of concerns, some of them psychological, some financial, some physical.

We consider what people feel about retirement, the way in which older employees see themselves and how others see them, their training needs, their caring responsibilities, and how their jobs and working environment are designed. In each case we consider how failing to meet older employees' particular needs can affect the quality of their work or even their ability to continue to work at all, and the loss to employers that this failure represents.

▬ Why should employers bother with older workers' needs?

If the needs of older employees are addressed, they can be opportunities. But if they are ignored, and older workers are lost to the business, this can lead to the worst of corporate crimes, waste – a failure to harness energy and a missed opportunity to respond to people who want to contribute, turning them into passengers instead of drivers.

Of course you can't waste talent that is not there. If an organisation has virtually eliminated older employees from its workforce, it can argue that it is not having to spend money on the potentially expensive needs described in this chapter. And yet that may be the greatest waste of all. When a business adds up the cost of reducing its workforce, the bill needs to include not only the cost in terms of redundancy and pension payments but also the loss of all that the company has invested throughout the career of each redundant employee, of all the skill and knowledge about the business that each employee has acquired.

W H Smith, with the help of the Institute of Manpower Studies (as it then was), researched the costs of replacing leavers. They took into account the costs of separation, temporary replacement, recruitment and selection, induction and training and concluded that the cost of replacing one sales assistant was £2,500. A 1 per cent reduction in staff turnover, they concluded, would save them £800,000 a year.[1]

■ Employees' attitudes to retirement
Retirement in prospect

It is of the utmost importance to employers that they are aware of how the people who work for them regard the prospect of retirement, and that they do what they can to help make those attitudes positive. Otherwise, the performance and contribution of a significant number of employees can be damaged.

In our discussions, we met a huge variation in employees' attitudes to retirement. People's views included:

- contented anticipation of the coming change in lifestyle and the opportunities that will go with it – in particular, enthusiasm about having more 'space' in life and an opportunity to get on with neglected interests and tasks;

- dread of the loss of structure, companionship, fulfilment and routine associated with work;

- anticipation of a welcome release from the negative aspects of work, for example tedium, stress and overwork;

- a view of retirement as a straightforward move from work to a well-earned rest or as an opportunity to turn to different forms of work, whether paid or unpaid;

- financial concerns – about inadequate pensions and, for many who retire early, the impossibility of replacing earned income.

Above all, prospective retirees are concerned about the unknown. The experience of retirement, though long awaited and predictable, is seen as a step into uncertainty.

Retirement in practice

For many people we spoke to, the experience has been very different from the expectation.

HEALTH

Perhaps the most surprising experience is the effect of retirement on health, both mental and physical. Although we may not recognise it, the routine of work produces for most of us a combination of exercise, mental stimulation, companionship, time structure and discipline, adjusted and developed over long periods, which serves us well. The sudden withdrawal of that routine through retirement, especially as it is often a subconscious discipline, is a real danger.

If it is not anticipated and managed well it can lead to depression, lack of fitness, serious illness and even death. It is a particularly important, and sometimes neglected, aspect of pre-retirement education.

FAMILY RELATIONSHIPS

The task of adjusting family relationships, especially with spouses, needs imagination, patience and foresight. 'Till death us do part – but not for lunch!' as one spouse famously put it. It is easy to offer advice in advance about alternative activity but for many newly retired people and their partners it will take quite a time to come to terms with such a huge change in the amount of time spent together.

Expectations may be very high – and dashed by experience and the stress on retired people who are for the first time in their lives separated from sources of advice and companionship. Retirement puts a heavy burden, not just on the person retiring, but on spouses and families as well; spouses, partners and other relatives often welcome the opportunity to join in the pre-retirement programmes which employers may offer.

VOLUNTARY WORK AND LEARNING

Individuals who opt for an active retirement often find a great deal of fulfilment, and a helpful form of continuity with the work environment, in both voluntary activity and learning new skills.

The research undertaken for the Carnegie Inquiry produced the curious finding that, in spite of the undoubted need for more volunteers, the proportion of retired people who do voluntary work is lower than the proportion of younger age groups. The reasons, which include lack of information and of confidence, are complex and not entirely clear; but there is plenty that employers can usefully do before retirement actually arrives to offer people advice and experience about volunteering. When the time comes they will then have a good idea of what is involved. We look at the opportunities for such help in Chapter 6 and in the case studies from BT and REACH.

Similarly, people who decide to learn new skills in retirement are often surprised at its relevance and its value in terms of building confidence and new contacts.

Employers need to be aware both of employees' concerns about retirement and of people's actual experiences and to take the trouble to find out more about them. If they do, and if they take the necessary action in response, they are much more likely to avoid problems of low morale and performance among older employees.

Gradual retirement

We found a frustrating gap between potential and practice in the area of gradual or phased retirement. We talked to many individuals who would dearly have liked to move gradually into retirement through a phased reduction of hours from full-time to part-time working over their last, say, five years of employment – with a corresponding build-up, while still in employment, of alternative activities.

The advantages for the individual are self-evident: the ability to try out new activities in advance, to reduce the fear of the unknown, and to make a gradual transition into retirement rather than seeing it as a sudden, cliff-edge prospect.

For employers too there are several potential gains, including the inherent flexibility of part-time working, the use of reduced weekly hours as a means of reducing labour capacity and the opportunity to retain the value of well-motivated and productive older employees who are preparing constructively for retirement.

In spite of the many advantages, the practice of gradual retirement seems to be remarkably rare. There are certain problems with Inland Revenue rules on drawing some but not all of a pension, if this is what the individual wishes to do. However, the biggest single obstacle is the theoretical incompatibility of this type of arrangement with pension schemes in which the pension is based on final salary.

If, for example, the pension is calculated, as many are, by applying a multiplier based on service (for example $\frac{1}{60}$th of salary for each year of service) to the best salary in, say, the final three years, the individual who has been working part-time for the final four years is clearly going to experience a dramatic reduction in pension.

Pensions experts regularly express surprise at the description of these difficulties and tell us that there are quite practicable ways round them. In some cases these are, or could be, incorporated into the rules of the pension scheme. They include:

- redefining final salary for pension purposes as the average of the best three years in the last five or even ten years, or the best single year in the last, say, five years;

- basing the pension on the individual's last full-time year;

- converting the period of service which is part-time into full-time equivalent service and then applying a full-time equivalent salary.[2]

However, the will of employers to find solutions to these problems seems remarkably limited when set against the potential benefits. Are the pensions and personnel policy managers talking to each other?

Job sharing by older and younger employees

In Wales we came across an example of an excellent plan to introduce a job-sharing scheme in which current full-time jobs would in future be shared between two groups of people: employees due to retire within three or four years and anxious to do so gradually and younger employees who for various educational, parental or other reasons would be pleased to be able to work part-time. Again there were substantial and obvious advantages, including a valuable means of transferring skills and knowledge. 'Sorry, can't be done,' said the experts, because of the pension scheme rules.

This seems to be a clear opportunity for employers and unions to do some innovative policy-making – from which everybody concerned would gain. In some European countries, other than the UK, the idea of combining gradual retirement with job-sharing schemes is being actively pursued by several employers. These include Volkswagen in Germany, TOTAL in France (the subject of a later case study; see p 105) and UAP in France.

UAP Phased retirement

UAP, the French insurance company, has used gradual retirement as a means of achieving a planned adjustment in the age profile of the organisation. It provides the option of differing amounts of part-time work in advance of retirement, with proportionate adjustments in salary. It has found that the system works best when it is adopted by a significant number of employees in a unit rather than by isolated individuals. It has also operated this arrangement for relatively senior employees.

Other companies in France operating gradual retirement arrangements include Hewlett-Packard, Rhône-Poulenc and Aerospatiale. Over 30,000 French employees were in gradual retirement schemes at the end of 1994.

In Sweden, just under half of all employees aged between 60 and 65 are in gradual retirement schemes. In Holland, there is a growing trend away from early retirement towards gradual retirement.[3]

■ Esteem and integration

Employers who are unaware of employees' concerns in their later years at work may pay a heavy price in morale and performance.

For too many employees, the last decade or so of their working life is a time of anxiety and frustration. Some are deeply fearful about whether they will continue to have a job at all, especially as they see their contemporaries disappearing around them. Some, as we have seen, are worried about retirement.

For others the worst aspect of their final years is a feeling of being unnoticed, unwanted and 'over the hill'. When they hear their company being described as 'a business for young people', when they become aware that they are no longer being considered for new jobs and projects, when they see training programmes excluding them and their older colleagues, it is no wonder that they start to doubt the organisation's regard for them. They may then find it very hard to see their work as providing fulfilment and enjoyment.

This type of behaviour by employers has little logic about it. It makes no sense to remove an older employee from consideration for appointments and promotions simply on grounds of age. The periods for which most managerial appointments last are relatively short, often no more than three or four years. Even when an employee's remaining years are limited, these relatively short chunks of service can be specially valuable in the process of succession planning, providing as they do the opportunity to bridge gaps until younger candidates mature and become available.

As we shall see later (see pp 80–81), assumptions about the decline of capacity in later years are rarely soundly based. Yet managers, we were frequently told, regularly use age as a short cut, as a proxy for making a proper assessment of an individual's potential performance, productivity and trainability. In practice, age is a very poor predictor of these qualities.

Illogical though it is, an atmosphere in which older employees are held in low esteem can easily and insidiously emerge in an organisation. When workforce reductions and early retirement schemes have diminished the sheer number of older employees, so that far fewer of them are actually about the place, that attitude is reinforced.

Redressing such an adverse view of older employees need not be complex or expensive. It can often be done by creating role models and setting examples. It takes only a few very visible appointments or promotions of older workers to demonstrate that a business does place a value on experience. And such appointments are not just signals: they are a real opportunity for importing wisdom, maturity and stability into a department or section which may particularly need those qualities.

Similarly, the inclusion of people of all ages in training and development programmes carries a clear signal from the employer as well as bringing diversity and experience to the programmes.

Such moves, together with good systems of advice and support for older employees which are designed to meet their particular needs (in just the same way as particular forms of support are necessary for new and younger employees), can bring about a remarkable transformation of the atmosphere. For individual employees the clear message will be that they are regarded as an integral and important part of the workforce, treated in most respects no differently from others and valued for their individual talents.

In one sense, our use of the term 'older worker' is misleading, suggesting the very stereotype which we have criticised. We do so only to highlight the concerns about the status quo. In an ideal world, there is no need for the distinction. As one participant put it to us, 'Some folks are old at 30, while others are young at 60.'

- Skills and training

Education and training can no longer be regarded as restricted to the young or those in their initial period of employment. The pace of technological change and the speed at which skills consequently become out of date mean that training should be seen as a constant need for all employees throughout their career, irrespective of age.

US evidence suggests that technological change and new knowledge requirements have reduced the 'half-life' of skills (the time it takes for workers to lose half their competence) from between 14 and seven years (depending on the occupation) to between five and three years over the last two decades.[4] Yet the evidence is that older employees are to a significant extent excluded from training. The Carnegie Inquiry found that:

- Nine out of ten older workers received no training in any one year.

- Among workers aged 35–59, 53 per cent of women and 44 per cent of men could not envisage any kind of training that they might receive in the next 12 months.[5]

Although this is not the direct responsibility of employers, older workers are also under-represented in Government-sponsored courses for unemployed people, even though unemployment affects older people disproportionately.[6] A survey sponsored by the Department of Employment concluded that 'most recruitment practices and programmes are designed for younger people and take no account of the potential of older people'.[7]

These low levels of training may reflect a perception by employers that there is likely to be too short a pay-back period to make the training of older employees worthwhile. But this ignores the evidence that labour turnover among older employees is lower than among the young. With young people increasingly moving between jobs, the period in which skills acquired through training can be put into effect is in practice likely to be similar for all age groups. Indeed, one report put it more strongly: 'A moment's thought soon shows that the 10 or 15 years of service which a 50-year-old potentially offers is considerably longer than the (say) three years for which a career-minded young employee is likely to stay with one organisation.'[8]

Some of the exclusion may be self-inflicted. Employees may regard themselves as 'too old to train' or may assume that they have nothing to learn at their stage of life. They may also be apprehensive about the training process and fearful about being in competition with younger colleagues who are more familiar with modern training methods and new technology. People do have a natural fear of being made to look foolish; much of the skill of the trainer lies in reassuring those who are learning that the experience can be enjoyable and fulfilling and that, rather than being competitive, those learning together can often learn as much from each other as from the formal teaching process.[9]

A further concern is that employees who are not regularly involved in training get out of the learning habit and find it that much more difficult to resume when the need arises.

If, on the other hand, individuals are encouraged to be constantly on the look-out throughout their careers for opportunities to broaden their skills and range of thinking, they will not only improve their employment prospects but also help to reduce the opportunity for age discrimination.

Older employees may need reassurance about the degree of skill likely to be required in a job. The vast majority of skills required by business are relatively straightforward. One research report suggested that 'most employees use more skill driving to work in their cars than they actually use when they get there'.[10]

Two of our case studies show how the process of learning at work is changing. Peugeot-Talbot's Assisted Development Programme offers all employees the opportunity to pursue courses on subjects of their choice, with the company footing part of the bill. In the UK, the motor industry – and the Ford Motor Co in particular – has led the way in introducing schemes of this sort. They were originally intended by the employers concerned to help in developing an atmosphere of learning and continual training – not necessarily of a vocational sort. They also enable employees to develop interests which they want to pursue in retirement.

Peugeot-Talbot Assisted Development Programme

The programme at Peugeot-Talbot was launched in 1991 and is available to all employees regardless of position, length of service or age. It gives them the opportunity to take up a course relating to a social, educational or sporting interest, with the company footing the bill up to £250 in any one year.

The programme was originally designed simply as a means of supporting employees in their entry or re-entry into non-vocational

hobbies, pastimes or interests. Twenty-five per cent of all employees took up the offer in the first year of the programme and this level has been maintained ever since, with about half that figure now representing newcomers to the programme each year.

Learning to drive and to play golf were initially the most popular courses. However, the programme has developed an excellent track record not only in these non-vocational areas but also in subjects of greater relevance to the company's own work. The next most popular courses are in computer studies and foreign languages – not insignificant in an advanced technology French-owned business.

More generally the programme continues to have an important benefit in encouraging an atmosphere of learning and continual training among Peugeot's employees.

Many of those taking part are older employees, encouraged to do so during the company's pre-retirement seminars. Examples of older employees who have enrolled are:

- a senior trade union official learning bookkeeping and accounts;

- a senior purchasing manager learning basic car maintenance and how to swim;

- a production worker (once a barber in Jamaica) taking an NVQ in hairdressing;

- another production worker learning football refereeing;

- a plant director studying water-colour painting;

- a production manager learning furniture restoration and carpentry. He said about his tutor, 'If my two grandsons were older, I'd leave them with him for five years to serve their time – that's the best I could do for them!'

The next case study describes Kvaerner-Govan's newly introduced adult apprenticeship scheme, which challenges the idea that all education and training has to take place at the beginning of a person's career.[11]

Kvaerner-Govan Adult apprenticeship scheme

Kvaerner-Govan (KGL) is a Norwegian-owned shipbuilding company with 1,800 permanent and temporary employees and based on Clydeside. In 1993 it was faced with a very practical problem: the new ships they were building demanded different skills. They had to re-balance their workforce to meet that demand and found that they were left with an unnecessary pool of semi-skilled workers.

Not wanting to lose around 300 years of accumulated experience, Kvaerner came up with a practical solution. The men would

become adult apprentices and top up their skills and qualifications alongside school leavers.

On the one hand, KGL's adult apprenticeship scheme makes all the sense in the world; on the other, it is a radical shift in big business policy, a new step forward for trade unions. It is overcoming the 'traditional' view of both apprentices and experienced workers.

All the men in question had been 'helpers' in the yard, working alongside tradesmen and skilled workers, in some cases for 20 or 30 years. KGL's Personnel and Employee Relations Director explained, 'These men were all committed to the yard, and to the industry. They had a vast amount of experience but would have had little prospect of finding another job if we had let them go.'

In January 1994, KGL started the men on their adult apprenticeship scheme. Fifteen new places were created (there has been no reduction in apprenticeship places for 16–17 year olds – currently over 50) and both generations of apprentices learn alongside each other as equals. Indeed, one father is following in his son's footsteps on the scheme!

The men's years of experience and existing skills are translated into 'credits' for their apprenticeship, and all are expected to complete the course in 18 months – half the normal three-year period – firmly knocking on the head the idea that ability to learn is dulled by age.

'The enthusiasm and commitment with which these employees have tackled their apprenticeship have made the training programme one of the most successful we have launched,' says KGL.

The trade unions, too, fully support the scheme. Davy Cooper, the trade union convenor, says, 'The game moves on, the issue was fully discussed at all stages, and now the adult apprentices are delighted. These men have been in shipbuilding all their lives. Now they are gaining new skills. They are useful people again.'

Swift changes and technological advances have put paid to the idea that you train once for a lifetime's work. People of any age can now retrain and pay back the company's investment. 'Five years is a long time in shipbuilding.' The adult apprentices will no doubt repay in full KGL's enlightened approach to training older workers.

Two more examples show innovative approaches based on a firm acceptance that learning must continue throughout our working lives.

National Westminster Bank Learning centres

National Westminster Bank is developing 'learning centres' throughout the UK which provide employees with ideas and resources to pursue their own learning. Age is not an issue in this encouragement of a learning atmosphere. The key objective is to make sure that everyone has the opportunity and the resources to allow them to take the initiative in assessing and meeting their own learning requirements.

Edinburgh University Open Minds scheme

The Centre for Continuing Education at Edinburgh University has introduced an innovative scheme called 'Open Minds' which aims to encourage employees from local businesses to enrol in one of the centre's hundreds of courses. This is essentially a local variation of the Assisted Development Programme operating at Peugeot-Talbot and other similar schemes, but in this case involving many different firms. Each participating organisation is given an individualised Opens Minds chequebook. Employees who want to join a course bring along a cheque signed by their employer as payment for the course. The employer decides on eligibility and the amount of subsidy, usually between £50 and £200 a year.

Our discussions pointed to two particular learning needs affecting older employees. First, they face a potentially punitive 'chicken and egg' dilemma: as we have seen, they tend to miss out on training, but without that training they are not able to compete in the labour market and are in danger of being sidelined even while they are still at work. Employers who make no discrimination on grounds of age in the provision of training are not only serving their own needs in the ways that we have described but also helping to counter the dangers of older people being trapped in long-term unemployment without access to the training they need for jobs.

Second, employers need to consider how well suited their means of providing training are to different categories of employee. There is no evidence to suggest that older workers learn less easily, but employers should bear in mind that in general they

- are less likely to have recent experience of education;
- are more likely to be questioning;
- tend to prefer to learn by 'on-the-job' methods rather than through fast-paced instruction in a classroom;
- prefer to 'self-pace' their learning;
- will respond to training methods which build on prior knowledge and experience;

- are valuable in and benefit from group activities – and may learn as much from colleagues as from teachers;
- can usefully act as teachers themselves.[12]

If learning is maintained throughout people's working lives, it is much less likely that they will become stale, unadaptable or rigid. The chances of atrophy through being in the same job for long periods (which is more likely to affect older workers) will also be reduced.[13]

There is an important cost aspect to learning: employers should consider the investment in training, induction and experience lost when an employee leaves a company, the corresponding costs which are incurred when a new employee joins, and the savings which are made by training an existing employee rather than recruiting a new one.

It may be, as one commentator recently suggested, that employers who can no longer offer total security of employment may need to think again about what they can offer employees by way of motivation and incentive. One answer may be 'security of employability': the knowledge on the part of employees that even if they have not got the certainty of secure jobs, they have got an employer who is willing to equip them with the skills which they may need in order to find employment elsewhere.[14] These thoughts are also reflected in the policy changes brought about in TOTAL in France (see case study on pp 105–106).

▪ Caring responsibilities

Responsibilities for dependent relatives are not of course peculiar to older employees, but the likelihood is that they will increase as employees grow older. Of the estimated 6 million carers in the UK, nearly half are aged between 50 and 74. One in five of those between 50 and 74 are carers. A survey by the charity Crossroads showed that 16 per cent of all people at work were carers, and that 18 per cent of these had taken time off in the previous month in order to care.[15]

A more recent survey by the Carers in Employment Group (see p 66) confirmed these findings and also found that:

- Many carers believe that employers are unsympathetic to their situation.

- Many complain of increased stress at work.

- Few organisations have any idea how many carers they have in their workforce.

- The flexible work practices which carers most request are time off for emergencies, flexible working hours, working from home and part-time work.

- Few organisations which do offer flexible working arrangements for carers monitor their take-up.[16]

There will be all sorts of different circumstances: the need to arrange constant care for an elderly and increasingly dependent parent, for a terminally ill spouse, for a disabled child. There will be emergencies and unpredictable demands. Some carers will have access to help from day centres, social workers and providers of respite care; some will find that help very hard to find; some again may not know about it.

For their working relatives, these people are a prime responsibility, whose care is usually undertaken with love and affection, often over many years and without recognition for their role being either sought or given. But employers need to remember that employees who are carers may be under intense pressure which they find hard to talk about at work. They may also fear that, if their caring responsibilities become known to the employer, their jobs may be threatened. It is too easy to dismiss this part of an employee's life as personal or domestic and no concern of the employer. Caring responsibilities are intensely demanding, and the people concerned may depend on being able to combine caring with working – partly for their own personal fulfilment but most importantly because they simply need the money.

There are real dividends for employers in understanding the needs of carers, bringing them out into the open and providing help in responding to them. The benefits will be seen not only in retention of employees who might otherwise have had to leave but also in reduction of stress and anxiety among employees, resulting in better performance.

This is an aspect of policy which, happily, some employers are starting to address, in recognition that there is mutual benefit for employers and employed in doing so. If employers do not allow the flexibility to enable their employees to combine caring with working, they will lose talent and incur the heavy additional costs of replacing the employees they have lost.

Marks and Spencer's recent introduction of a new family care policy is a good example of an employer responding to these needs.

Marks and Spencer Family care policy

Marks and Spencer have long recognised the importance of providing conditions of employment which encourage staff to stay with the company and to aim for long-term careers. For this reason, the company in 1990 introduced fully paid maternity leave, child breaks and the option of part-time working for management staff. These provisions have now been extended to larger numbers, including supervisory staff; they involve 18 weeks' fully paid maternity leave, child breaks of up to five years' unpaid leave, and the option of working part-time for three years following maternity leave and then reverting to a full-time contract.

M & S have recently extended these arrangements, which were widely welcomed, to include dependency leave, to meet the needs of employees who become responsible for caring for a dependent relative. The policy acknowledges that the attempt to combine working and caring can lead to stress, absence from work and a decline in work performance. The company has also recognised that with increasing numbers of older people in the population and with home care now becoming more common, there is likely to be a growth in the number of M & S employees who are carers.

The new dependency leave arrangements are available to all categories of staff with over two years' service who have responsibility as the principal carer for an elderly or disabled relative or a sick child.

Staff in these circumstances are first invited to change to a pattern of part-time work which suits their caring responsibilities. If this is either inappropriate or impossible, the individual can take between three and nine months' unpaid leave. This period of leave will be regarded as continuous service by the company.

If at the end of this period of unpaid leave the person concerned requires more time off to deal with caring responsibilities, a break from employment of up to five years can be given. During this period benefits cease and the period concerned does not count as continuous service, but the individuals concerned are guaranteed a position with the company on their return.

An important first step for an employer developing this type of policy is to find out how many people there actually are in the workforce who have caring responsibilities. This should be done in a way which preserves the anonymity of carers, which can be a very sensitive issue, and which makes clear the purpose of the survey – namely to identify needs for policy development.

Another useful approach is to use focus groups of carers within the business, who can bring direct experience of the issues concerned and the views of fellow employees within the context of their own particular business.

The key requirements of carers themselves are for recognition and flexibility. Carers need to know that their employer knows about and understands and accepts the implications of their responsibilities and is willing to respond 'to them. If specific policies are in place, there is no need for employees to be fearful of being 'found out', or of their prospects being damaged if their caring responsibilities become known.

Flexibility is essential because, by their nature, roles are constantly changing. Carers need:

- to be able to work part-time to match the availability of other help;
- to be able to adjust their hours as circumstances change;
- to be able to respond to emergencies;
- to have a place of work reasonably near to the relative they care for and to be confident that they are not going to be transferred to a remote location.

Finally, there are services which an employer can provide at the workplace, as part of such a policy, which will help the carer to combine the two roles without undue damage to either – for example access to a telephone during the day to check if there are any problems and information about local sources of help.

Another case study from Peugeot-Talbot is about an exciting plan to provide a day centre for the dependent relatives of employees.

Peugeot-Talbot Day centre for dependent relatives

This initiative is still at the planning stage and much remains to be done to turn it into a reality, including raising the money. However, there is considerable excitement in Peugeot-Talbot about the idea of establishing a day centre for elderly people.

The background is an inexorably growing problem which particularly affects older employees. With an ageing population and an increasing number of frail elderly people, there is more and more need to provide care for people suffering from conditions such as Alzheimer's disease, who may well need continuous attendance and support.

These responsibilities often fall on older employees, who find it difficult to get respite care to enable their spouses or partners to get out and do the shopping, have a day off – or indeed go to work in the knowledge that their parents or other elderly relations are being properly looked after.

Working with BEN (the benevolent association for the motor industry and its allied trades), Peugeot has designated a small redundant office block at its Stoke plant to be developed as a workplace day centre for elderly people.

With BEN providing the necessary professional care, and with the involvement of employee or retiree volunteers to assist the professionals, the idea is that elderly relatives, not just of Peugeot employees but of anyone working locally in the motor industry, could be picked up and brought to the centre, perhaps by their sons or daughters on the way to work, perhaps by a volunteer. They would spend the day under professional supervision, with activities available during the day including handicrafts, having their hair done, having chiropody treatment or simply socialising – perhaps alongside fitter, more active pensioners who might just drop in for lunch or a cup of tea and a chat.

The plans are being supported by the Peugeot-Talbot retired employees association, which has experience in running its own daytime club and in organising bingo, tea dances, daytime trips and other social events.

From the company's point of view, the plan, which has good support from employees as fundraisers and potential volunteers, has the advantage of encouraging better attendance and reduced turnover of staff, through giving employees confidence that their relations can be looked after in a secure and supportive environment.

Policies for carers in employment should be monitored regularly to see whether they are meeting the needs of employees and of those they care for, to encourage ideas and feedback from carers, and to help adapt and improve arrangements.

Of course there are limits to what an employer can do by way of flexibility, but there is a world of difference between regarding caring duties as no concern of the employer and, on the other hand, talking through in advance what can and cannot be done against the background of a positive policy which recognises carers' needs.

An important development is the formation of the Carers in Employment Group by the Princess Royal Trust for Carers. The group is an alliance of organisations concerned for the welfare of working carers. It was launched in 1995 with a valuable survey of 23 organisations and it is the source for some of the suggestions and information outlined above.[17]

▬ Job and workplace design

If employers are to succeed in making the workplace attractive to older workers, and in retaining them in employment, another aspect which they will need to look at is the design of jobs and places of work. There is little evidence that employers have addressed this task with the needs of older workers specifically in mind, but here is another example of action for older workers which is likely to benefit all. Issues to look at include:

- the distances and heights through which objects have to be lifted;

- the space needed for working (research in France suggests that older workers do not generally take longer to do tasks or find them more difficult provided that their needs are taken into account in the way the job is organised. The research showed, for example, that woodworkers over the age of 50 operated just as effectively and fast as younger workers but that they had a greater need for working space in order to maintain the necessary equilibrium in their working positions[18]);

- the amount of repetitive action needed;

- lighting and heating;

- insulation from excessive noise;

- the length of time for which employees are required to stand;

- seating design;
- the positioning of working surfaces and VDUs.

Employers' action points

EMPLOYEES' ATTITUDES TO RETIREMENT

- Do you know how your employees view retirement?
- Can your employees retire gradually – by reducing their hours of work from full-time to part-time in their final years – without damaging their pension?

ESTEEM AND INTEGRATION

- Do you know whether older employees in your organisation feel anxious, fearful or frustrated in their final years of employment?
- Do your managers make too many assumptions about the capacity and potential of older workers?

SKILLS AND TRAINING

- Are training opportunities open to all your employees, regardless of age?
- Have you thought of supporting employees in furthering their own education and of what this might do for the process of learning in your business?
- Have you thought about helping employees to acquire the skills which they may in due course need in other employment?
- Have you thought about whether older employees may need any different training methods or about using older employees as trainers themselves?

CARING RESPONSIBILITIES

- Do you know how many of your employees care for dependent relatives?

- Do you know whether carers in your business are worried about combining working and caring? Are they frightened to let it be known that they have these responsibilities?

- Do you know how much absenteeism because of caring may be affecting your business?

- What do you think you could do to help carers? What do you think they want? Have you asked them?
  Time off?
  Part-time work?
  Understanding?

- Do you monitor the take-up of any facilities which you do provide?

JOB AND WORKPLACE DESIGN

- How much thought has your business put into the design of the workplace?

4 Age and equal opportunities

In this chapter we look at age discrimination in relation to other forms of discrimination. We ask how serious a problem it is; we distinguish fair and unfair discrimination; we look at the various types of age discrimination and consider the reasons for it. We ask whether younger people should be given preferential treatment. Finally, we consider the arguments for and against legislation, and the action needed by employers.

▬ Ageism – the odd one out?

Discrimination on grounds of gender and race have become familiar, high-profile issues for our society. Both are seen as social evils, recognised first by campaigners and then by successive statutes.[1] Public distaste for acts of discrimination on either ground, whether in employment or elsewhere, has become natural and widespread. Any employer knows the perils, if not the folly, of allowing any such discrimination in the workplace, in terms of both penalties and damage to reputation.

This is not to say that these problems have been overcome. No one can be satisfied with progress until there is full representation of both ethnic minorities and women at all levels and roles in our society. Ethnic minorities experience higher rates of unemployment and hold less skilled jobs than white people, while women are under-represented in senior and managerial jobs, as well as in Parliament. (While women represent 45 per cent of the labour force at work, only 20 per cent of managers are women, 7 per cent of senior executives and less than 1 per cent of chief executives; 9 per cent of MPs and 7 per cent of Members of the House of Lords are women.[2])

In November 1995, the Disability Discrimination Act received the Royal Assent. Among other provisions, the Act, when it comes fully into effect, will give individuals who believe that they have been discriminated against on grounds of disability the right to complain before an industrial tribunal.

This is a welcome development and a very necessary one, given the problems encountered by successive governments in promoting employment for people with disabilities. But it has another significance. The newest of the discrimination statutes means that three of the four major types of discrimination are now regulated by law. But the fourth, discrimination on grounds of age, remains the odd one out – with no legislation, no commission charged with addressing it.

For those affected by ageism, the unfairness, indignity and frustration are no less – and yet we have got nowhere near the same acceptance that this, like any other form of discrimination, needs to be eradicated.

It is worth remembering, before we look at these issues more deeply, that every one of us is potentially affected by this form of discrimination. This is not to belittle the problems posed by other forms of discrimination or to suggest that they should be given any lower priority. But we will all be either dead or old at some time. It is ironic that the one cause of discrimination which can affect every one of us is the one that has been given the lowest priority by legislators and employers alike.

This is not just a moral issue for employers. The business case for equal opportunities in general is becoming gradually better understood. Employers who have developed positive equal opportunities policies have not done so just because they have been on the receiving end of a moral crusade or because in some areas they have been compelled to act by law but also because they have seen real business benefit in getting access to the widest possible pool of talent.

Age needs to be on the same agenda – for the same reasons. Sloppy, stereotyped thinking and short cuts in personnel systems have no place in a business which wants to make the most of a diverse workforce with a good spread of age and experience. And because everyone is potentially affected, the knowledge that a business may be treating older employees less favourably than others can easily influence the morale of the whole organisation.

Although we are concerned in this book with older workers, and thus particularly with discrimination against them, it is not only older people who are affected. We now hear regularly of people in their 30s and 40s who are told that they are too old to be considered for vacancies. Assumptions are equally made about young people purely on the grounds of their age: that they cannot have the necessary abilities for a job simply because of their age.

▬ How serious a problem is it?

In all its forms, age discrimination is widespread:

- Age limits are still widely used in recruitment advertising: samples of newspapers and journals have shown proportions of advertisements with overt age bars ranging from 11 per cent to 41 per cent.

- This is more likely to occur in the private than the public sector, in advertisements for white-collar rather than blue-collar jobs, in advertisements placed by agencies rather than by employers themselves, and in advertisements placed in the *Sunday Times*, *Daily Telegraph* and *Financial Times* as opposed to the *Guardian*.[3]

- Upper age restrictions are placed in 8 per cent of vacancies notified to Jobcentres (though more place a lower age limit than an upper one).[4]

- 83 per cent of unemployed workers who are 45 or over believe that their age will hamper their efforts to find another job; 7 per cent think that they will never work again and only 3 per cent see their age as being no barrier. [5]

- Nine out of ten employees over 50 receive no training in any one year.[6]

- In a survey across Europe seeking views on the extent of age discrimination, the UK was the member state in which the highest proportion of respondents believed that older workers were discriminated against in employment – whether in recruitment, promotion, status or training.[7]

- Discrimination is not just experienced by people over 50. In one of the excellent guides for local authorities on older workers produced by the Metropolitan Recruitment Agency (METRA), the author quotes evidence that people who leave their jobs to gain a degree through full-time study experience age discrimination at 30; that women wishing to return to paid employment or to change their jobs face discrimination at 35, and that men start facing discrimination at 40.[8]

Nor is there any evidence from the experience of individuals that age discrimination is decreasing. A November 1995 survey by one of the largest UK outplacement agencies found that three-quarters of the 237 individuals surveyed believed that age discrimination was on the increase; two-thirds said that they had been excluded from job interviews because of their age. The average age at which respondents thought that job prospects started to become limited was 42, and 79 per cent felt that employers did not give due regard to the experience that comes with age.[9]

- Fair and unfair discrimination

It is not discrimination in itself which is misguided and wasteful. After all, choosing a person to do a job is essentially a process of discriminating between several people. In its literal sense, discrimination is a process of choice and in that sense there is nothing wrong with fair discrimination. Indeed it is the employer's responsibility, and not always an easy one, to choose or discriminate between candidates for recruitment, promotion and even redundancy on the basis of ability to do the job best.

What matters is that the grounds for discrimination should be objective and justified. Injustice and waste occur when the grounds for discrimination are unfair and based on needless assumptions and when they take into account factors such as gender, race or age which are nearly always completely irrelevant to ability.

▪ Discrimination in recruitment

The most familiar form of discrimination is in recruitment. Employers seem to have much more negative attitudes towards older applicants for jobs than towards older existing job-holders. Sometimes the discrimination is overt – when, for example, employers include specific age limits in recruitment advertisements. A quick glance at the vacancies columns in the daily and Sunday papers will confirm that many employers are still doing this.

What is so special about a process engineer between 28 and 35? A corporate lawyer who must not be over 38? The reasons, if there are any, are never made clear. It is hard to understand why employers should assume that people outside those age brackets do not have the necessary skills – and harder still to know why they should want to deprive themselves of half the available talent. Occasionally, there are some welcome words in an advertisement making it clear that age is not an issue or that candidates of all ages are welcome, but this is still quite rare.

During 1995, as part of the Carnegie Programme, we wrote to over 500 of the largest employers in the UK asking them to agree, if they had not already done so, to abandon the use of age limits in recruitment advertising and also inviting them to confirm that age was specifically included in their equal opportunities policies. The level of response (120 replies – just over 20 per cent) was disappointing and of itself indicative of how far we have to go, but the results from those who did reply were instructive and encouraging.

▪ Nearly 90 per cent of those who replied told us that they do not or will not use age limits in recruitment advertising, or only do so in exceptional circumstances, for example to meet insurance requirements (eg requiring employees with driving responsibilities to be over a certain age).

- Over 80 per cent of those who replied told us that they either now have, or will in future have, equal opportunities policies which address discrimination on grounds of age.

At the same time, we approached 104 employment agencies who had published advertisements for jobs containing age limits, inviting them to question any instruction by a client to include age limits and to agree not to initiate such limits themselves. The results were again instructive.

- 33 per cent of those who replied agreed to commit themselves to the two suggested actions.

- 30 per cent agreed with the suggested actions but indicated that there would continue to be circumstances in which their clients would require reference to age.

- 15 per cent justified the use of age limits, in some cases admitting that this was to reduce the number of applications.

It is encouraging that the majority of those that responded agreed with the suggested actions. The exercise has also played a part in getting the message across that this is a practice which is almost always unjustified and increasingly rare.

It is interesting that in our monitoring of the use of age limits in job advertising, we did not come across a single example of their use in the public and voluntary sectors.

Employers wishing to avoid age discrimination might usefully ask recruitment agencies acting and advertising on their behalf:

- not to use age limits simply as a means of cutting down the number of applicants or as a criterion in shortlisting candidates;

- not to specify age limits unless the client has specified them;

- if there are specific reasons for focusing on a particular age group, such as complying with insurance requirements, to explain those reasons openly in advertisements;

- not to use age limits as a proxy for other qualities assumed to be associated only with younger candidates, for example potential, energy, dynamism;

- not to assume in shortlisting candidates that managers making appointments will automatically want to appoint only people younger than themselves;
- to have a comprehensive equal opportunities policy governing work on behalf of clients and to include age as an issue within it.

One employer we spoke to makes a practice of including its equal opportunities policy, which rules out the use of age limits, in the procurement agreements it makes with recruitment agencies and requiring them to agree to abide by the terms of the policy in any work done for the company.

Indirect or covert discrimination is just as significant. Advertisements may, for example, say that a job is 'suitable for a young, dynamic candidate'. They may refer to a business as 'a young person's company'.

Even if the process of advertising does not seek to exclude older candidates, it is of course very easy for an employer to operate an age bar in sifting out the responses to advertisements. We know from our discussions with individuals that this is a widespread practice.

We met many people in their 40s and 50s who were deeply frustrated at their inability to get beyond the initial disclosure of their age. Several sought advice as to whether they should conceal their age, and at least get to the first stage, or even lie about their age – and risk being discovered.

It may seem surprising that ordinary, adult people should even think of deceiving employers in this way. What most of them are evidently saying is that they are determined to find some way of showing the employer that they have got at least as much to bring to the job as a candidate within a specified age bracket, if only they are given the opportunity to present themselves.

Covert discrimination of this sort is one of the reasons why legislation is not a simple answer to the problem; it might be very hard indeed for a complainant to prove that an employer had sifted out all applicants over 50.

We came across a number of examples of employers who had decided to abandon the requirement for the date of birth to be provided in application forms. The general principle should be that information on the age of employees is required only for the purposes of monitoring. Where age information is required for this purpose, it should be made clear that this is the only reason why the information is needed. The explanation of this in employment documents can be a useful vehicle for getting the message through that age is not otherwise relevant.

When recruiting, employers may place more emphasis on background and educational qualifications than they need to determine whether an individual is competent to do the job in question. Bearing in mind that older people tend to have lower qualifications than their younger counterparts, this may in practice mean that older people are unfairly barred from consideration. (Two-thirds of those between 50 and state retirement age left school at 15 compared with one-third of younger adults; two-thirds of those who are today between 50 and 74 have no qualifications, compared with only 18 per cent of those in their 20s.[10])

The next case study describes an excellent initiative by the Employment Service in the north-west of England.

The Employment Service — Competency-based recruitment

The Employment Service in the north-west has been involved in an important pilot scheme in recruitment to its own ranks. The scheme, which has now been adopted as standard recruitment practice in the Service, was designed to show the advantages of systems of recruitment which are not based on traditional 'proxies' for competence such as age or academic qualifications but rather aim to assess people on their true worth.

The Employment Service is a major employer in its own right, running the national network of Jobcentres and Unemployment Benefit Offices. It employs some 42,000 people and is thus regularly involved in quite substantial recruitment.

It is strongly committed to pursuing equal opportunities for everyone in its recruitment and employment practice. This is spelt out as meaning that it treats all applicants for employment and employees fairly, irrespective of their ethnic origin, sex, marital status, sexual orientation, age, religion or disability.

The Service became an Executive Agency in 1990, as distinct from an integral part of the Employment Department, and has thus acquired the freedom to develop its own recruitment and other policies to meet its own business needs, rather than automatically applying standard Civil Service procedures.

The Service is particularly concerned to ensure that its selection and recruitment methods are fair and open and enable it to recruit the right person for the right job. This is important not only in making sure that recruitment is as effective as possible but also because it acts in many ways as a role model for other employers throughout the country. The Service is also determined to ensure that the recruitment procedures which it recommends to its clients are in operation within its own organisation.

At each stage of the recruitment process, applicants are assessed on the basis of their ability to carry out the job for which they have applied. The process aims to focus on actual skills rather than background or formal qualifications.

In order to make sure that it receives applications from as wide a base as possible, the Employment Service's job advertisements specifically encourage applications from 'disadvantaged' groups. Thus it targets inner city residents, people from ethnic minority backgrounds and older workers – all groups of people who might well have believed that they were not eligible for employment by the Service or likely to be accepted.

A change of particular significance is that the Service has dropped the traditional Civil Service practice of requiring academic qualifications of various sorts and levels as a condition of consideration for employment. Instead, each candidate is asked, through a combination of the application form, work samples and structured interviews, to demonstrate in other ways that he or she has the skills appropriate for the job.

The candidate is given the chance through the application form to describe and demonstrate skills gained in any area of life, whether from work, school, voluntary work or home. The decision as to whether to invite the candidate to the next stage of selection is made primarily by reference to the skills section of the form.

If the candidate is asked to go to the next stage, the next requirement is to take part in a series of written tests lasting about an hour and usually held at one of the Service's local offices. These tests are based on the tasks which will be undertaken by successful candidates.

Thus candidates for an administrative post will be tested on numeracy and use of English. Candidates for advisory or supervisory positions will be tested partly on the basis of their ability to take in the contents of a real Civil Service information circular and to answer questions to check their understanding of its contents.

These written tests often form part of an 'open day', when the candidates have the chance to meet real people carrying out the kinds of jobs for which they themselves have applied. Selection is a real two-way process, with both parties learning as much as possible about each other.

The next and final stage for those who succeed in the written tests is an interview carried out by two or three people, usually members of the management team concerned. The interview concentrates on establishing whether there is a good match between the competencies required for the job and the qualities and skills described in the application form and subsequently tested. The requirement is to make a fair and objective assessment of the skills and abilities actually possessed by the candidate and to avoid making assumptions from other, extraneous factors.

Applicants are encouraged to amplify the information provided at earlier stages and to make the best possible case as to why they believe that they are right for the job.

Candidates who are not successful may be asked if they would like to go on a waiting list, with the possibility of an offer of a suitable job at a later date, so that the effort put into the process is not wasted.

The Employment Service places great emphasis on retention of good employees once recruited through these methods and has found that this is much enhanced by investment in induction, probation and training.

These changes in recruitment practice have been fully evaluated and monitored, with feedback from both recruits and managers. The results have confirmed the effectiveness and value of the new systems. In a recent recruitment exercise in the north-west in which the Service was seeking to fill some 60 posts, 1,033 applications were received and 64 people were offered employment, of whom an unusually high proportion – 33 out of the 64 – were over 45.

The Service regards these changes as a major success in showing to employers generally the advantages which can be gained from freeing up the recruitment process and not artificially discriminating through traditional prejudices or assumptions based on, for example, age or qualifications.

There will of course be a few jobs – increasingly few – in which the necessary physical strength, stamina and agility are more likely to be found among younger people. But even in those cases, for example in heavy manufacturing or in some parts of the motor industry, it is better to test individuals for the necessary qualities than to assume simply from their age that they cannot do what is required.

Employers often instinctively or deliberately follow employment patterns based on a vertical career – involving recruitment of young people and promotion from within – and an assumption of long service. As we have already seen, these patterns are rapidly disappearing. Yet the habits of recruitment die hard and may militate against mid-career recruitment and opportunity.

▪ Other forms of age discrimination

The same stereotyped attitudes towards age and experience are likely to stand in the way of older people being promoted to vacancies and being included in training programmes and may even affect the way in which their pay is determined.

It takes only a little reflection to see that excluding older people from training makes little sense. As we saw in Chapter 3, they need to have their skills updated in just the same way as everybody else. They bring to training courses a very welcome addition of experience and maturity – so much so that experienced trainers will often use them as part of the training process.

Today, with rapid and constant changes in technology, skills become outdated at a much greater pace. Employees of 50 may well need to learn and relearn skills and techniques several times in the final 10 or 15 years before they retire. Why assume that they are less capable than younger people of doing so?

Another form of discrimination involves employers using age as a basis for selection for compulsory redundancy – although a recent industrial tribunal case held that this was tantamount to unfair dismissal.[11] In Chapter 5, we look more closely at how workforce reductions have been targeted on older workers.

Hardest of all to deal with, and particularly damaging to morale and so to business, are the unconscious forms of discrimination. They are more likely to occur, for example, when the numbers of older people in a business are steadily reduced through workforce reductions focused on older people – whose very absence produces an unspoken culture of low esteem for experience and age. Employees who remain may well be encouraged to believe that older people have no place in the workforce. If the vast majority of employees are under a given age, their experience of what people over that age have to bring to the business will go on diminishing – and they can never value what they have not known.

▪ Reasons for discrimination

Our discussions suggested that discrimination does not generally occur as a result of deliberate malice or prejudice, but rather as a result of a quite complex set of different attitudes which combine to form an often unconscious but nevertheless potent exclusion of older people from opportunities in employment. They include:

- stereotyped and usually unwarranted assumptions about the capacity of older employees. This leads to a tendency to generalise about their capacity rather than assessing them on an individual basis;

- the association of youth with energy, dynamism and creativity and an assumption that these qualities decline with age;

- an undervaluing of the skill, experience and maturity that come with age;

- an assumption that older people do not need, do not want or are less able to be trained

- an assumption that older candidates will want to command more expensive remuneration packages;

- an assumption that they are likely to be more prone to short-term absences.

Manpower reductions targeted at older people will tend to reinforce prejudices because older workers are no longer there in force to demonstrate their value.

There is also the possibility that relatively young and junior personnel staff, to whom the responsibility for large-scale recruitment is often entrusted, may recruit in their own image. Those making appointments to jobs which report to them may also be reluctant to appoint people older than themselves, for fear that their own competence and authority may be challenged by people of greater experience (this was confirmed more than once in our discussions with recruitment agencies).

The irrationality of most of these pretexts is self-evident. Research for the Carnegie Inquiry found that:

- There are likely to be more differences within age groups than between them.

- Age does not necessarily lead to loss of competence. To take a simple example, the copy-typing speeds of individuals do not in practice reduce as they grow older and their accuracy actually increases.

- Any decline in mental and physical capacity (which is much more likely to occur after normal, let alone early, retirement age than before) will in most cases be offset by gains in experience and expertise, so that overall competence is generally not affected.

- Contrary to stereotyped thinking, labour turnover is actually lower among third agers than among their younger counterparts (one of our employer participants told us that, on average, people in their 40s and 50s stayed with them four times longer than people in their 20s).

- The incidence of short-term sickness is no higher among older employees.

We know that many older people are quite content to take leadership and direction from younger people, to take on different, more flexible and sometimes less responsible jobs as they approach retirement, and not necessarily to seek constant growth in seniority and remuneration.

It is possible to reverse many of these attitudes. Research for the Institute of Personnel Management (now the Institute of Personnel and Development) tells the story of a public sector organisation which made real efforts to break down recruiters' assumptions that age hierarchies should match organisational hierarchies and that it was (possibly mutually) unacceptable that older people should be recruited to positions in which they would be subordinate to younger ones. Those involved reported that it was partly because of the steps they took to counter these assumptions that they felt that age was no longer a major issue in their organisations.[12]

The case study on B&Q in Chapter 2 summarises that company's experiment of concentrating employment on older people. A more detailed study of what happened at B&Q found that many of the assumptions made about older workers were misplaced. Older employees, they found, tended to be more committed and mature in their work, directly contributing to higher standards of customer service. No significant differences in productivity were discovered and, although some were slower than others, this was at least compensated for by the greater likelihood of older employees getting things right first time and the lower risk of accidents resulting from their being more conscientious and careful. Relationships with younger workers were good, particularly when, as often happened, older employees assumed 'mentoring roles'.[13]

But the discrimination persists – and no one should doubt that it is deeply entrenched. One of the most disheartening aspects of all our discussions was the consistency with which people were being excluded from consideration for employment long before employers had had a chance to consider the merits of the individual candidates concerned.

Researchers also suggest that there is a correlation between difficulty in recruitment and employers' acceptance of older workers: the harder it is to recruit, the greater the acceptance of older workers. Older workers have been referred to as a 'buffer zone' for employers, used when there are labour shortages but not retained or recruited when there are labour surpluses;[14] last in the queue when employers need more labour but first in the queue when surplus labour needs to be shed.[15]

We sometimes heard it said, for example in the motor industry, that an organisation could not employ older people because the jobs were too physically demanding. Too often this seemed to be applied far more widely than was justified. Even if there is quite a high proportion of manual jobs which are less likely to be suitable for older employees because of the physical demands they make, this should not lead an employer to conclude that there is no place for older workers elsewhere in the organisation. Indeed, the case for such employment is all the stronger if the business as a whole is to maintain a good age balance.

▪ Should younger people be given preference in employment?

There is one pretext for discrimination against older people which may be seen as having greater foundation, and is therefore worth considering in more detail. This is the view that we met quite often in our work: that in times and places of high unemployment, younger people should be given preference in employment over older people who have had their chance – and that encouraging employment for older workers may be at the expense of the young. Several points need to be made in response.

- First of all, none of the Carnegie work seeks to promote a campaign for older people in preference to younger. What we have consistently argued for is a level playing field, on which all candidates are considered on their merits.

- A workforce which is restricted to employees of any age group will fail to include the different qualities which result from a good and balanced age profile: combining experience and maturity with energy and vigour; memory and knowledge with flair and creativity; loyalty with ambition; toughness with courtesy. Employers need all these qualities. While they should never assume that they are the prerogative of particular age groups, which would be discriminatory in itself, they are much more likely to achieve them if they ensure that they recruit and promote from all age groups.

- Older and younger employees are not necessarily in competition with each other for jobs. Younger candidates may be more likely to seek full-time, permanent jobs, whereas older people may prefer part-time, temporary and flexible employment. As a recent ILO report points out, 'new entrants into the labour market often lack the experience necessary for the jobs vacated by older workers'.[16]

- Looking at the economy generally, if older workers retire from the workforce, especially during a recession, they are lost permanently. Next time the economy picks up, labour shortages and inflationary pressures will emerge that much sooner, and on go the brakes. As a result, the economy will run at a lower level and the number of available jobs will be reduced.

- It is a mistake to think of there being a fixed volume of work to be shared out. Economies do not work like that. This 'lump of labour fallacy' ignores not only the fluctuation of the labour force to reflect consumer demand but also fluctuation to meet the availability or otherwise of employees with different characteristics.

It is just as unfair to rule out older candidates simply on grounds of their age as it is to do the same to younger candidates. There is room, and need, in the economy for people of all ages, with their different characteristics and contribution.

▪ Paying for future retirement income

There is another important economic reason why we need to avoid excluding older people from work. With the population ageing and the number of people at work static or reducing, there will be a growing financial load on people at work to pay for the state pensions of the retired population. In 1971, there were 28 people of pensionable age for every 100 people of working age; by 1991, there were 30, and by 2030 it is estimated that there will be 47.[17]

The size of the retired population is being affected by two factors working in combination. Not only will the numbers be swelled by the future retirements of the baby boom generation; those larger numbers of people are also going to be living much longer and therefore requiring retirement income over a longer period.

This is not a problem which is exclusive to the UK, and it calls for major policy decisions by governments about how to share the responsibility for providing retirement income equitably and effectively between state, employer and individual. One of the best ways of ensuring that the responsibility of the individual at work is limited to what is reasonable is to enable older people who want to work to do so. And yet, through the various forms of age discrimination which we have discussed, we are actively excluding them.

This is not an argument which employers can stand back from and ignore. If they are not addressed by everyone who contributes to retirement income, the consequence will be higher taxes and insurance contributions for all.

(Figures obtained from the Government Actuary for the Carnegie Inquiry show a stark picture: the state pension is today (1995) equivalent to 16 per cent of male average earnings. If present policies on price indexation are maintained, and on reasonable assumptions about future economic performance, the pension will be equivalent to 9 per cent of average earnings by the year 2030. To maintain the pension at its present level of 16 per cent would require an increase in the level of National Insurance contributions (NICs) from the present 19 per cent joint employer's and employee's contribution to 26 per cent. To produce a better pension value than 16 per cent would clearly require even higher NICs.)[18]

▪ Government policy and legislation

Employers need to be aware of Government policy and potential in this area for two reasons. First, they may be directly affected by Government action, whether through legislation or through the action of Government agencies and departments. Second, the actions of Government may well be influenced by the conduct of employers. If employers are to be credible in resisting calls for legislation on this or any other subject, they need to show by their own actions that it is not needed.

In spite of the extensive age discrimination which we see happening all around us, there is no legal constraint on it – although, as we have seen,[19] age-based selection for redundancy has been found to be unlawful and an age limit affecting a greater proportion of one sex than another can amount to indirect discrimination under the Sex Discrimination Act.

The policy of the present Government is to favour a voluntary approach. In 1993 Ann Widdecombe, then a Minister at the Department of Employment, launched a campaign to highlight the unfairness of age discrimination. It seeks to persuade employers, personnel professionals and decision-makers at all levels of the value of older workers and to demonstrate the benefits of policies which allow people of all ages to contribute to the success of their employers. The campaign also encourages older workers themselves to be positive about the range of skills and knowledge they have to offer.

An Employment Minister (Mrs Cheryl Gillan at the time of writing) also chairs an Advisory Group on Older Workers. It consists of 12 men and women who have a wide experience of industry and of the problems of age discrimination in employment. With the help of the Advisory Group, two booklets have been published to reinforce the message that age has no bearing on the ability to do a good job. *Getting On*, published in 1994, is aimed specifically at employers and illustrates the benefits to any organisation that can result from abandoning age discrimination in recruitment, training and retention. *Too Old . . . who says?* was published in January 1995 and contains a wealth of help and advice for individuals seeking employment, changing jobs or training for new skills.

At a regional level, the Department of Employment has organised a series of seminars designed to disseminate good practice in the employment of older workers among locally invited employers.

The 'Getting On' campaign set out five positive steps for employers to take:

- drop age bars;
- select on grounds of ability;
- welcome older applicants;
- offer flexible working;
- invest in all workers, regardless of age.

In its own work through Jobcentres, the Government's Employment Service seeks to dissuade employers from including age limits in job advertisements. If they insist, the Jobcentres still send them applicants who fall outside those age limits and often those apparently ineligible candidates are appointed.[20]

The policy of the Labour Party is 'to expand existing anti-discrimination legislation and provide new opportunities for removing discrimination on the grounds of race, sex, disability and *age* in recruitment, promotion, redundancy and retirement for men and women up to the age of 65'.[21] More recently (in September 1995), the Party confirmed its intention, if elected, to introduce comprehensive legislation against age discrimination, including providing a right to complain of age discrimination before an industrial tribunal.

The Carnegie Inquiry preferred a voluntary approach but concluded that, if employers failed to demonstrate that they were capable of dealing with the problem without compulsion, then there would have to be legislation.

There are several powerfully expressed arguments against legislation on this subject – including what is seen as the limited success of such legislation in those countries which have it.

In the United States, for example, even after 25 years of operation of the Age Discrimination in Employment Act, Congress regularly declares that statutory protection against age discrimination remains incomplete and somewhat ineffective, for example in reducing the proportion of older people among the long-term unemployed.[22]

On the other hand, those who have lived with it comment that the US legislation – which is comprehensive, covering recruitment, dismissal, promotion and benefits – has had a strong impact. One of our participants, returning from a period of working in the USA, commented that the exclusion of information on age in employee records got him out of the habit of considering how old people were. One American study concluded: 'Human resource executives will admit that unlawful age discrimination remains. They assert however that the [Age Discrimination in Employment] Act and the sometimes significant liability that it has authorised has greatly reduced the incidence of age discrimination in employment.'[23]

The USA is not the only country to regulate age discrimination. In France, age limits in recruitment advertising are banned. Several Australian states have comprehensive age discrimination legislation. Some regulation also exists in Austria, Canada, Germany, Greece, New Zealand and Spain. In Ireland the government has announced that a current review of anti-discrimination legislation will be used as a basis for introducing age-related protection in the future.[24]

Employers and their organisations have argued for years – in relation to employee participation and industrial democracy, control of hours of work and most threats of regulation of employment – that better results are likely if employers are convinced of the importance of acting voluntarily and through self-interest than if they act under compulsion. It is a line of argument which puts a heavy onus on employers to prove their credibility through action.

Other reasons for opposing legislation on this issue are that it would involve an expensive enforcement bureaucracy, that it would be hard to frame effective regulation, that covert discrimination would be hard to prove, and that regulation might simply remove the most obvious forms of discrimination without dealing with the bulk of the problem.

US experience suggests one possible perverse result of regulation. One consequence of the US legislation, which among other provisions prohibits dismissal on grounds of age, has apparently been a rapid growth in offers by consultants of 'assessment processes' designed to find other grounds of selection for dismissal than those blocked by discrimination legislation.

The other side of the coin is that the history of race and gender legislation in the UK tells us very clearly that a milestone of major importance in the battle against both those forms of discrimination was the passing of legislation. It does not always take the application of the law to produce the desired effect. The knowledge of and publicity for sanctions against employers has clearly had a strong deterrent effect. The very existence of the law makes a statement on behalf of us all, through the parliamentary process, that this is a standard of conduct which we expect to be followed. For many employers it takes no more than that to persuade them to act.

If we are to go on accepting the argument for a voluntary approach, we need powerful reasons why employers should act without compulsion – and one of those reasons can be the threat of legislation. However, the pressure to act is less if there are no means of monitoring whether progress is actually being made. If targets are set and it can be shown whether or not good practice is spreading and progress is being made, well and good. But if there is no monitoring and if legislation is ruled out at any time, then there is little pressure on employers to take the subject seriously.

Although the voice of employers against further regulation is a strong and understandable one, it is interesting that it is not universal. A survey of employers conducted by the University of Sheffield produced a majority in favour of legislation: 53 per cent in favour compared to 37 per cent against (the balance were either don't knows or did not reply).[25]

The respondents were predominantly personnel managers, and the message may be that they need the strength of the law to give them the authority to put this type of discrimination on the same footing as other forms – perhaps because their masters are not ready or willing to give them that authority, or do not see the issue as a priority.

However, a more recent survey of managers of all types and sectors confirmed the same support for legislation. Of 370 comments on the statement 'Legislation should be introduced to outlaw ageism in employment', 67 per cent either strongly agreed (38 per cent) or agreed (29 per cent), 16 per cent were neutral and only 17 per cent either disagreed or strongly disagreed. A larger-scale survey from the same source to be published in Spring 1996 confirms this level of support for legislation, with an even larger proportion favouring a ban on age limits in recruitment advertising.[26]

In our own discussions, we met many managers whose views on the subject faced both ways: they were reluctant to see greater regulation of their affairs but at the same time doubtful as to whether age discrimination would ever be given the same treatment and priority as other forms without that powerful, visible statutory message.

▪ Integration in equal opportunities

Irrespective of the case for or against legislation, our discussions revealed widespread support for a more integrated approach to equal opportunities, both within businesses and on the part of Government. The existing legislation has developed on a piecemeal basis, and is continuing to do so with the most recent legislation relating to disability. This means that there are three separate agencies dealing with discrimination on grounds of race, gender and most recently disability, different bases of operation for each, and separate statutes for each cause. There is no statute or agency concerned with age. The situation seems expensive and unsatisfactory.

Even if age continues to be the odd one out in respect of legislation, there is a strong case for both employers and Government to adopt an integrated approach. As one employer put it, 'Employers cannot afford to take a fragmented approach to equal opportunities; why should Government do so?'[27]

As things stand today, employers are on the receiving end of a series of mixed messages, issued at different times, with different emphases and from different sources, on the various types of discrimination. This does not present the powerful, coherent message about the need to eradicate discrimination in all its forms that is so badly needed. We also heard in our discussions of many experiences of multiple discrimination, for example against older black women and older disabled people.

The Report of the Commission on Social Justice suggested that Government should consider the case for a single law prohibiting unjustified discrimination, which could be enforced and promoted by a single Human Rights Commission, rather than trying to develop a series of separate anti-discrimination laws.[28]

Although it might have to operate through a series of specialised divisions, there is evident merit in the idea of a single statute making it illegal to discriminate on any ground and a single agency charged with addressing and monitoring discrimination in all its forms and presenting a strong business case for a diverse and varied workforce.

▪ Action by employers

A major step in tackling age discrimination and addressing issues of age generally is simply to ensure awareness of the issue within an organisation. In our discussions we asked employers whether they were aware of the age distribution of their workforces, of the average ages of those in their employment and of trends in age composition and the implications for future staffing. Interestingly, those that were aware of these things were in a minority.

The majority were aware of general trends in average age – usually that it was reducing as a result of voluntary early retirement programmes. Few could easily put their hands on age profiles or any more detailed information related to age.

The extremes in attitude and policy in this respect are represented by two examples.

Bradford City Council Annual staffing profile

Bradford City Council produces and publicises an annual staffing profile, updated quarterly, which displays in easily understood charts a complete profile of its employees. It shows the composition of those employed not only by age but also by ethnic origin, full-time/part-time work, salary, recruitment, gender, absenteeism, disability and labour turnover – each shown both in terms of the whole workforce and department by department.

Not only is this profile visible to all in the council's employment and in the community, it is very much a feature of policy planning. The employer regularly sees and assesses the profiles, including the 19.2 per cent of staff aged 50 or over, what this represents in terms of the skill, experience and maturity of the workforce, and how it is likely to be affected by policy options under consideration at any time.

Age profile (April 1995)

Age	Number
Up to and incl 19	494
20–29	4,186
30–39	6,619
40–49	7,771
50–59	3,823
60 and over	701
Total	**23,594**

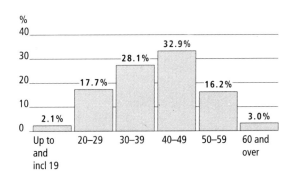

This is not to say that this type of information is not available in other organisations. If you dig deep enough it usually is. The key points in the Bradford case are that the information is public and that it is used.

The other extreme is represented by a comment made in a gathering of personnel directors comparing notes on the subject of age: 'We still have 2,000 people over 50!' The clear implication of the comment was that it was almost something to be regretted or ashamed of that these people had not yet been ejected from the organisation, that the residual older employees were seen as something of an anachronism and that the employer concerned was fortunate to have this last remaining 'cannon fodder' to use for future redundancies.

Figure 1 Age and gender profile of the workforce

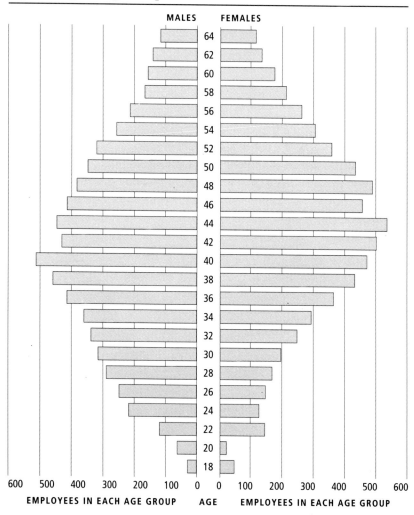

In mainland Europe, wide use is made by employers of the 'demographic pyramid' – a simple graphic means of representing simultaneously the age and gender profile of an organisation. Figure 1 provides an example, with the vertical axis for age and the horizontal axis for numbers of employees. Males and females are shown to the left and right respectively of a central vertical line.

Figure 2 Age and gender profile of the workforce

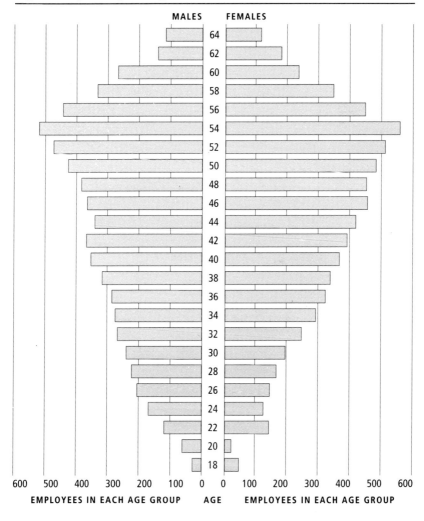

Although this method of presentation is familiar to demographers, it is not yet widely used by human resources managers in the UK. It is useful, not just as a snapshot presentation of the various issues involved but more importantly as a guide to the likely trends over the years, to the consequences of unchanged policies and to the possible effects of new policies.

Figure 3 Age and gender profile of the workforce

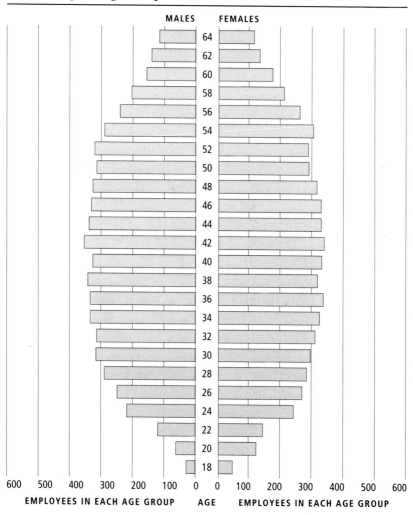

For example, a profile which today looks roughly like a rugby football (as in Figure 1) will, given unchanged policies, gradually turn into the shape of an upside-down Christmas tree (Figure 2), representing the dangerous future prospect of a dramatically reduced number of older employees coupled with a shortage in the supply of younger workers. The analysis may carry important messages – particularly the need to implement employment policies sooner rather than later and to anticipate these problems and to act on them before it is too late.

I recently asked a representative of a major French employer which makes regular use of such charts as part of its personnel planning what shape an ideal profile would be: a rugby football, a globe or circle, or perhaps even a sausage (Figure 3). He rapidly stressed the limitations as well as the value of the device. It was no more than a tool, he said, and the idea of an ideal profile was illusory. Its value was for monitoring and testing the effects of possible future policies. However, he conceded that a cylinder or sausage-shaped profile was probably healthier than an inverted Christmas tree.

An organisation's commitment to addressing these matters can be valuably and publicly demonstrated by a clear policy statement; this is especially effective if it covers not only the commitment but also the rationale behind it. The Post Office's policy statement provides a good example:

The Post Office: Equal opportunities statement

Equality of opportunity is an important part of good management and crucial to producing an effective organisation. We are totally committed to making full use of the talents and resources of all our employees, current and potential.

No employee will receive unfair or unlawful treatment due to race, colour, nationality, ethnic or national origins, religion, creed, sex, sexual orientation, marital status, or disability, nor face unwarranted discrimination on grounds of age.

W H Smith has gone further and has produced a 'Group Statement on Age', with four supporting principles. Of particular interest is the way in which it aligns the company's employment policies relating to age with its commercial and business objectives.

W H Smith Group Statement on Age

The goal

Our goal is to develop and sustain a workforce profile that reflects the age structure of the community we serve through effective and efficient human resourcing, and to seek opportunities through recognition of the current and future trends in the age profile of the population.

The guiding principles

1 We will respond positively by reflecting the changing age profile of society in our employment practices and in the development and delivery of our products and services.

2 We acknowledge that, despite increasingly positive views, older workers still face significant stereotypes. We are working to remove age discrimination in all aspects of employment as an integral part of our equal opportunities goal.

3 We believe that employment decisions based on age are rarely justifiable and lead to ineffective use of human resources. Within our business, we continue to challenge the use of age and age-related criteria in every aspect of employment decision-making.

4 We want experience and work-based achievements to be valued as much as academic qualifications. We want the ability to do the job rather than formal education or qualifications to form the basis for our selection decisions.

The message is clear: adopt and publicise a clear statement of policy, know your age profiles, monitor the trends, and value and preserve the element of maturity and wisdom represented by the right-hand side of the Bradford chart.

If employers are to succeed in making sure that age is firmly on the equal opportunities agenda, they need a comprehensive programme of action to that end. The suggestions set out in the employers' action points at the end of this chapter build on the checklist for action produced by the Institute of Personnel Management (now the Institute of Personnel and Development) in 1991 and revised in 1993 to form the Institute's Statement on Age and Employment.[29]

In 1995, the TUC took the welcome step of issuing guidance for unions on age discrimination, both in selection for redundancy and more generally. It urges unions to negotiate agreements with employers which refer specifically to older workers and to examine conditions of employment and collective agreements in order to identify provisions which may discriminate against older workers, including redundancy and early retirement schemes.[30]

Employers' action points

- Do you have a policy on equal opportunities which addresses all aspects of discrimination, including age, in an integrated way?

- Do you use the experience you have gained in addressing discrimination on grounds of race and gender to tackle issues of age discrimination?

- Are you satisfied that your employment conditions do not include unnecessary age-related criteria in any area, including recruitment, selection for training, counselling, development, promotion, determination of pay and selection for redundancy?

- Do your employment forms, including recruitment application forms, ask for information on date of birth?

- Do your recruitment advertisements include age limits?

- Have you communicated your policy on age discrimination and equal opportunities to recruitment agencies who act on your behalf (for suggestions see p 74)?

- Can you find opportunities to demonstrate the organisation's policy by visible and prominent appointments, including appointments of people of all age groups?

- What are you doing to break down assumptions that subordinates must be younger than those to whom they report?

- Are systems in place to ensure that individuals are matched with jobs purely on the basis of their skills, knowledge and competences?

- Do you monitor the composition of the workforce by age and trends in the average age of employees? Have you considered publicising the results of monitoring?

- Are you satisfied that older employees are not excluded from training programmes?

- Have you thought of appointing a senior person in the organisation with responsibility for implementing and monitoring the equal opportunities policy?

- Have you considered taking positive initiatives to increase the proportion of older employees in groups where they are under-represented?

5 Workforce reduction and older workers

We look now at how action by employers to reduce the size of their workforces has particularly affected older workers, and at the use of voluntary early retirement and what it has meant for employers and employees. We reflect on the price that employers may have paid for focusing on older people in this way and we look ahead to future policies for workforce reduction and their impact on individuals

▪ Voluntary early retirement

It is now hard to find an employer left in the UK who has not reduced employee numbers substantially in the last five years and has not done so by focusing on older workers. Throughout Europe, there are now many businesses where early retirement is not just an option but the norm. In some cases there are few if any employees at all who are over 55 – or even 50. The scale of reduction has been huge and yet has attracted relatively little public comment.

Most of the reductions have been achieved by some form of 'voluntary' early retirement – in contrast to the redundancies of the early 1960s and 1970s, when the principle of 'last in, first out' was widely adopted by employers and advocated by trade unions as the most equitable basis of selection for redundancy.

Why has this change come about? In our discussions we came across six separate possible reasons for such a major change in attitude and policy.

The wishes of employees and trade union members In the earlier period, people seemed to place a higher value than today on long service and continuous careers. Today's employees seem to accept that they will retire earlier and that periods with one employer will be shorter. A recent survey by a large trade union (MSF) covering over 420 workplaces and 140,000 workers showed that 74 per cent of respondents wanted to retire before the age of 60, a further 20 per cent when they were 60 and only 2 per cent at 65.[1]

Ideas of fairness, growing concern about youth unemployment and a view that those who are nearer retirement have less to lose. As we saw in Chapter 2 (see p 36), it appears, for better or for worse, that people in the UK are now likely to have much shorter periods in one job than people in other developed countries.

Changes in trade union influence, although the targeting of older workers in this way has not generally been against the wishes of the unions. Indeed, in most cases it has been with their collaboration in preference to compulsory redundancy.

Cost factors and the perception by employers that older workers are more expensive. The costs of funding older workers' pensions in final-salary-based schemes are higher because the length of service of older workers is generally greater and the level of pay higher. It was reported recently that the pension costs to a company of a 30-year-old represent about average company pension costs (5 per cent), whereas the pension costs of those over 50 are on average three times as much.[2] On the other hand, there is often a heavy cost to a pension scheme in providing the enhanced pension element of an early retirement programme. If pay is age-related, then that is again a cost consideration – but the practice of relating pay to service, as opposed to performance and the rate for the job, has declined very significantly in the last decade.

The growing prosperity of pension funds Many pension funds have been in surplus in the period in question because of a combination of favourable investment circumstances and the changing structure of employment and pensioner numbers. Employers who have included voluntary early retirement schemes in their redundancy programmes have often been able to arrange for the pension costs of those schemes to be covered from their pension funds rather than from their ordinary revenue.

The deep concern of both employers and unions to avoid compulsory redundancy – on the face of it an understandable and familiar motive.

Most organisations have offered terms which have been attractive enough to bring forward sufficient volunteers to achieve the required reductions. In some cases, the offer has been oversubscribed. In 1992, for example, when BT was seeking 30,000 volunteers for the first of its 'Release' schemes, of which voluntary retirement was the principal ingredient, 44,000 applied for release.

Most retirement schemes have involved a combination of:

- payment of an immediate pension for those over a defined age, usually 50 or 55;

- the granting of additional, notional years of service;

- some form of lump-sum severance payment based on the service of the individual.

Terms such as these have proved compellingly attractive to many. Some employees with long service have found themselves better off when retired early than if they had stayed in employment.

On the other hand, an approach which is described as voluntary – and is voluntary in the sense that the employees affected make a conscious decision to opt for the terms which have been offered – may not in reality involve a free and easy choice. Employees have inevitably asked themselves whether they dare refuse the terms offered, either because of uncertainty as to whether they would be offered again or for fear that later reductions might have to be handled through compulsory redundancy, perhaps on less favourable terms.

Employees may also underestimate the cost of early retirement in erosion of the value of their pensions. For many, pensions will be increased only to a limited extent, and their pension after 20 or more years of retirement will be very substantially lower than if they had stayed in full-time or even part-time work and continued to make contributions. Many are dependent on state benefits by the time they are 60. Research suggests that employers' arrangements for retirement planning and counselling do little or nothing to increase employee awareness of these dangers.[3]

■ Individuals' experience of early retirement

We decided, as part of this project, to look more closely at what the experience of voluntary early retirement has meant to the individuals affected.

It is perhaps too easy for employers to make assumptions about the motives of people opting for early retirement, about their actual experiences when compared with their expectations, and about the process of making the choice and the support needed in doing so. Information about this aspect of employment, or departure from it, is not widely available or up to date.

The results of the survey which we conducted through the Institute of Employment Studies in the summer of 1995 into the experiences of some 1,700 individuals who had retired before normal retirement age since 1991 are set out in Appendix 2. The individuals concerned met with a huge variety of experiences, which we hope will be useful to employers in shaping their policies for similar actions in the future.

Early retirers survey **Summary**

Some have gone gladly, with the opportunity and resources to pursue their own personal interests. Some have taken up voluntary work. A minority have found alternative paid employment, with many finding it far harder to achieve alternative employment than they had expected.

Many have been dismayed and shaken by the experience of moving from the structure and security of paid employment to meet for the first time unemployment, prejudice against older people, isolation and limited support. Some have experienced serious personal hardship. Many have experienced the reality of age discrimination when seeking alternative work or even opportunities for voluntary work.

Problems faced by local authorities

Local authorities across the country have faced a particular problem in achieving workforce reductions as a result of a legal decision in 1992 involving North Tyneside Council.

North Tyneside Council Voluntary severance terms

With the aim of bringing about a significant reduction in staff, North Tyneside Council decided to include within a package of voluntary severance terms not only enhanced pensions payable immediately to staff aged 50 or over but also, for all employees affected, one-off severance payments in excess of the statutory minimum redundancy payments laid down by the relevant statute (the Employment Protection (Consolidation) Act 1978).

This decision was legally challenged in a case which went to the High Court and finally to the Court of Appeal. It was ruled that under the terms of the Local Government Act 1972 the Council was legally barred from exceeding the statutory minimum payments.[4]

This decision has meant that, until recently, any local authority reducing its staffing, and wishing to do so without resorting to compulsory redundancy, has effectively had to rely solely on early retirement, with the features likely to attract volunteers being limited to enhanced pensions payable immediately to those aged 50 or over. Younger employees have had little incentive to volunteer and in consequence local authority reductions have been significantly weighted towards older employees – with the now familiar consequences of distorted age profiles and loss of skill and experience.

Some relief against this restriction is being given to authorities in the context of the current round of local authority reorganisation, but for many the damage has already been done.

Benefits and costs to employers

Although they have rarely been described as such, the staff reductions we are considering have represented for employers a huge but effective investment. The one-off costs of funding the various redundancy schemes have been met from reductions in operating profit, often allowed for through special provisions in company accounts for this purpose. Sometimes, as we have seen, they have been supported by contributions from their pension schemes.

Employers themselves may not have equated this expenditure with other more recognisable forms of investment, but there is no doubt that the expenditure involved is likely to be recovered many times over by a massive and permanent return in terms of the employment costs which are saved.

In weighing that return, however, we must – perhaps with the benefit of hindsight – put into the balance costs which were probably not anticipated when the redundancies were planned. These are not easy to measure and certainly need to be brought into the reckoning in planning future reductions.

The price of early retirement

Employers have been learning the hard way that the benefits of avoiding compulsory redundancy though early retirement schemes have been offset by a heavy price in terms of loss of skill, age balance and experience.

This side of the balance was clearly of concern to Sir Brian Pearce, at the time Chief Executive of Midland Bank, when he exclaimed in a television interview, 'What have we done to ourselves? Where are all our grey-heads?'[5] As another senior manager put it, 'We have thrown away the memory of our business!'

We suggested in an earlier chapter that a modern business is essentially its people and the expertise, knowledge and contacts which they possess. Does it not follow that it is at best foolhardy and at worst a form of self-mutilation to cut back on numbers in a way which seems specifically designed to cut out those very qualities?

If we look at any organisation which has carried out reductions in this way, we repeatedly see several particular causes for serious concern:

- too many individuals just biding their time until they reach the critical age of 50 or 55 when they will qualify for the early retirement package. This becomes a collective milestone for older employees – some looking forward to it, some dreading it – with the business as a whole coming to regard those who remain after that age as exceptions and oddities;

- reduced performance and productivity from employees fearing, awaiting or deciding on early retirement;

- a reduced regard for the wisdom and value of experience, not for any logical reason but because there are so few people left to exemplify these qualities;

- a stepping up of pressures on those who remain, with less time left for thinking, planning and reflection, and a tendency to work ever longer hours;

- an unconscious and self-fulfilling attitude towards older employees that if they could be spared through these schemes, they could not have been of great value;

- a growing inability to learn from experience because the people who could have pointed to earlier projects and lessons learnt in the past are no longer there;

- a mismatch between the age profiles of the employees and customers of the business;

- an absence of the mature and stabilising influence of an older generation of employees, able to help younger colleagues to see their frustrations and pressures in context;

- distortion of arrangements for succession planning when such a large slice of the workforce is not available for consideration. And yet, as we have seen, the older individual, with a defined and limited period of service available before retirement, can represent an invaluable chunk of resource to include in a succession plan before an identified younger person is ready and available for the post in question;

- the loss of one half of the pairing of older and younger employees in one of the most effective forms of teaching and learning – 'sitting next to Nellie'.

Our participants also commented on the dangers of regarding early retirement as a cheap option. Many were familiar with the funding of early retirement packages through pension funds and the tendency to regard the costs to the pension fund as somehow different – or not even as a cost at all. Of course the costs are no different from any other: at the end of the day they will be at the expense of employer and employee contributors to the pension fund.

TOTAL, the major French oil company, provides an informative example of a business which has made substantial changes in employment policy following earlier reductions in staff based primarily on older workers.

TOTAL New policies on age profiles

In the 1980s TOTAL, like many other European employers, addressed its cost and competitiveness problems by encouraging early retirement and a substantial slowing down in the recruitment of younger people. The result has been what they describe as 'an unbalanced demography', the principal feature of which is a high proportion of 40-year-olds in the management population generally and in many individual establishments. This position conflicts with the company's continuing need to tackle competition and achieve permanent increases in productivity.

TOTAL accordingly decided

- to resume recruitment of junior staff, both to provide motivation for staff generally and to enhance the perception of career opportunities;

- to move away from the position where it was becoming the norm for people to end their careers in their 50s;

- to develop the idea that employment should be to a much greater extent managed by the individual rather than by the company management;

- to end the practice of encouraging large numbers of people over 50 to leave the business;

- in parallel, to introduce the opportunity for gradual retirement combined with job-sharing, with older employees transferring to part-time work and sharing their jobs with others, whether younger or older. This has had two aims: first, to reduce the number of work stations in the company without necessarily reducing the number of employees and, second, to help get away from the idea of one person per work station;

- to encourage mobility in employment, in both geographical and functional terms, so that it becomes the norm for employees to adapt constantly throughout their careers, varying job content and skills, places and types of work, developing professionalism and questioning established habits of work.

TOTAL has taken two other initiatives as part of this redirection of policy. The first is the introduction of a system known as 'rendezvous d'emploi' or 'career meeting points'. This reflects the company's view that, if a business can no longer offer people a permanent career, it should instead give them a greater say in shaping their own careers and in the acquisition of skills. The rendezvous system offers to all employees at the end of their second or third major assignment within TOTAL, at around the age of 45, an in-depth interview with a consultant, examining options for the next stage of their career.

The purpose is to explore preferences and to discuss future opportunities appropriate to the individual, both within the company and outside it. An analysis is completed by the consultant and this is then discussed by the employee and a senior manager of the company within the normal appraisal system, but with the added advantage of the consultant's report.

The second initiative has been the establishment by TOTAL, together with other major French employers, including Aerospatiale and Rhône-Poulenc, of the Passerelle Association. The aim here is to provide opportunities for the employees of these major companies to be seconded for short periods to small and medium-sized businesses so as to gain an awareness of methods, issues and projects other than those of their own employer, and a greater familiarity with the business world beyond the horizons of their own employment.

The Passerelle scheme has been popular and successful both with the major employers involved and with those companies to whom their employees have been seconded. The involvement of several major companies means that they are much better equipped to meet the wide range and volume of requests for secondments.[6]

▬ Looking ahead

No employer can look ahead to a time without pressures for reduction of costs. Many businesses know that for several years ahead they will be continuing to reduce employee numbers. Sir Brian Pitman, Chief Executive of Lloyds Bank, for example, has been reported as warning that 75,000 further jobs – one job in five – are likely to be lost from the banking industry in the next five years.[7]

If our comments about recent use of voluntary early retirement schemes as the principal means of reduction have been critical, it is because many of the employers we spoke to have acknowledged the shortcomings of what they have done. There are no easy ways (apart from so-called natural wastage, and some of that is painful) of reducing employee numbers without pain – though employers have sought, in various ways, to reduce that pain.

As we look back on the reductions of the late 1980s and early 1990s, we may well come to see them as part of a distinct phase – different, as we have seen, from the 'last in, first out' period of the

1960s and 1970s but different, too, from what will have followed in the late 1990s and at the start of the new century.

The next period is bound to be different, if only for one simple reason: many businesses have far fewer employees aged 50 or over, as successive waves of older employees have been removed by repeated applications of voluntary early retirement. As we look ahead, we can therefore expect to see employers seeking new methods of reducing employee numbers. Not all of them need involve putting people out of work, as the following examples from British Airways and Volkswagen show.

British Airways Alternatives to redundancy

British Airways needed to reduce the capacity of customer service staff in one of its units at Heathrow Airport. Instead of the familiar approach of cutting out whole jobs, the company offered the staff concerned a series of choices about different ways of working. These included:

- taking voluntary unpaid leave of absence for anything between one month and one year – with pension contributions maintained, service treated as unbroken, and the employee free to take other employment in the period of absence;

- taking a career break for a longer period, up to three years. This involved leaving the company and the pension scheme and being free to apply for vacancies at any time within the break, but without a guarantee of re-employment;

- transferring permanently to part-time working;

- switching temporarily to part-time working – for a minimum of two years with a transitional payment of six months' pay;

- for employees over 50, switching to part-time work until retirement – with pension contributions based on part-time pay but a pension based on full-time pay, and a transitional payment of six months' pay (reduced pro rata if employees had less than two years to go till retirement).

These choices were available to staff on a voluntary basis and were taken up on a sufficient scale to achieve the necessary reduction in capacity without full-scale redundancies and without anyone becoming unemployed as a result.

Volkswagen Reducing capacity by working shorter hours

In 1993, when Volkswagen in Germany was faced with the need to reduce production and costs, management and workforce agreed to cut the working week from five days to four, with a corresponding reduction in pay, in order to prevent redundancies. A year later, when the company needed to increase output and wanted to enlarge its workforce again, it found that many of its employees no longer wanted to return to full-time working.[8]

The Commission on Social Justice also noted that all vacancies in the German government sector are now open to those wishing to work part-time or to share a job, as well as to full-time workers.

But part-time working can deal with over-capacity only to a limited extent. Inevitably, future reductions will cost whole jobs and employers will continue to search for the fairest and least damaging means of choosing who has to go.

Not many organisations will be able to achieve the reductions that are still to come by continuing to rely on a supply of willing volunteers for early retirement. Not only have most of the older employees already gone; the lessons of lost skill and experience have, we hope, been learned and the costs paid. For some organisations it will take years to restore a satisfactory age balance in their workforce.

Future redundancies are more likely to be achieved through policies which ensure that, once the necessary reduction has been achieved, the business is left with the combination of skill, experience and knowledge of the business which is required for its future prosperity and survival.

An anonymous employer Alternatives to voluntary early retirement

A recent article gave an account of an un-named company making parts in the automotive industry.

In considering redundancy policies arising from a restructuring, the company vigorously rejected selection for redundancy based on age, describing it as 'an irresponsible waste of human resources, inefficient and a danger to the jobs of other employees'. Instead, they introduced a policy of compulsory redundancy that retained the best employees. This not only increased the quality of the workforce but maximised the chances of the remaining workforce having a future with the company.

This switch from earlier policies based on voluntary redundancy initially met with resistance from management, staff and trade unions. However, a major effort was made to communicate the reasons for the change; support was gained by getting across the message that, in a situation in which everyone could lose their jobs, the company had to retain the best employees.[9]

■ Attitudes of ex-employees

Organisations must decide how they want their older employees and ex-employees to regard them.

If people are treated reasonably, positively and with understanding by their employers, even in the process of parting company with them, they can be good ambassadors for their former employers. And there are many such ambassadors around. But employers have to earn that regard by working out the needs of older employees and people who are leaving and providing good support arrangements for them.

Alternatively, people will be angry because they have been undervalued, ignored or rejected because of their age. If they have been treated unfairly and harshly, they will not forget it. There are also many of these angry people around, and hundreds of them have identified themselves during this project. They have no remaining respect for their former employers and they can seriously damage organisations and their reputation.

Nothing can adequately compensate individuals who lose their jobs unwillingly, but there is quite a lot that an employer can do to ease the process and to help people adapt to new circumstances, acquire new skills and find new employment.

Financial compensation is by no means the only way in which employers can help to cushion the blow of redundancy: it is possible to anticipate some of the circumstances in which surplus employees are likely to find themselves and to provide them with appropriate support.

The story of the huge reduction in its workforce which BT has brought about – over 100,000 since 1989 – is a significant example.

BT Release packages

Starting in 1993, BT introduced a series of 'Release' packages. In addition to the familiar ingredients of severance payments, voluntary early retirement and pension enhancements, these included a 'menu' of additional benefits from which employees could choose, according to their own circumstances and preferences. This menu was developed in response to employee comments and experience since 1993. Its final package for 1995 included:

- support for people wanting to start their own business – including training, help with preparation of a business case, and equipment at discounted prices;

- a self-help package, including job-search information;

- career consultancy and outplacement support for people seeking to take up a new career;

- training to acquire new skills;

- a programme for people over 50 not wanting to continue in full-time work but needing help in preparing for retirement;

- support for people interested in working for voluntary and community organisations. This builds on an earlier programme called Skillbase in the Community, which is the subject of a case study in Chapter 6.

All these additional benefits have involved cash payments of up to 10 per cent of pay to support the individual in making the particular type of change involved.

BT was able to announce in 1995 that, through a succession of company-wide schemes, including these additional elements, it had achieved the bulk of the large-scale manpower reductions which it needed, that any future reductions would be limited and localised, and that it no longer needed to undertake company-wide reductions through further Release programmes.

In developing their policies, employers need to ask themselves what they want their former employees to say about them:

'Once they had decided to get rid of me, they just didn't give a damn. They just wanted me out quickly and to be able to forget about me. Frankly, I couldn't wait to go.'

Or:

'I have to say that I was very reasonably treated. I was sorry to go as I enjoyed my job but the terms I went on were pretty good and I got real help from the company. They actually thought about me as an individual. I don't mind giving them credit for that.'

The words are real – and so is that choice for employers.

Employers' action points

- If you have used voluntary early retirement as a means of workforce reduction,
  Are you concerned about the effect on the age balance of your workforce?
  Did you anticipate the loss of skill and experience involved?
  Are your customers concerned?
  Do you know what has happened to the people who took early retirement?
  Even if you want to, will you be able to rely on early retirement for achieving further reductions?
  Has the loss of older employees affected attitudes to those older people who remain?

- If you are planning to reduce the size of your workforce in future, what is the relative importance of achieving the reduction on a voluntary basis and maintaining the most effective workforce following the reduction?

- Is redundancy the only way of achieving the reductions you need?

- Have you considered offering people shorter hours for less pay, on a temporary or a permanent basis?

- What additional measures can you take to help reduce the impact of redundancy on individuals:
  Help with finding new employment?
  Help with acquiring new skills?
  Help with preparing for self-employment or starting a new business?
  Help with preparation for retirement?
  Introduction to voluntary work and volunteering opportunities?

- Have you considered what people who leave your organisation on redundancy terms think about the business when they have gone?

6 The transition to retirement

In this chapter, we discuss the process of moving out of work and suggest why an employer should be concerned to support it. We look at the special needs of employees in their final period of work and ways in which they can be helped to prepare for their next move; at pre-retirement planning; at links between older employees and the community activities of organisations, and finally at the relationship between employers and those who have retired.

▬ Why should employers bother to offer support?

Every career involves a series of transitions: into work, through its various elements, and towards and into retirement. All our discussions confirmed the view that the transition from work to whatever follows is a time when positive employer support can make a real difference. If handled well, the process of retirement can be straightforward and full of opportunity. But it can also bring with it stress, disappointment and frustration.

Why should employers bother with helping employees to make these transitions? Surely, when resources for supporting employees are limited and under pressure, there must be doubts about devoting any of them to people who will soon be gone from the business for ever?

Most of the organisations we talked to took a different view. The reasons why they put considerable effort into helping employees to prepare for retirement included:

- their concern to be regarded by present and future employees as 'good employers', with the reputation of addressing employees' needs at all stages of their careers;

- the knowledge that ex-employees who have been thoughtfully supported in the process of retirement or even redundancy are likely to be good ambassadors for the business for many years to come – and vice versa;

- the recognition that employees who feel neglected, apprehensive and insecure during their final years of work are going to be less productive and far less capable of bringing to bear the special qualities of wise counsel, maturity and stability which they have to offer.

Charles Handy tells us that British businessmen, when pressed for their real purpose in life, nearly always say that they want to make their pile and then do something 'which really interests them'.[1] The same applies in different ways to people at all levels of seniority. Surely it makes sense to help them, if only because they will be happier and more productive at work if they can take a positive view of what lies ahead.

There is a danger of thinking of employees' needs only on the eve of retirement. We need to start earlier. Many employees, as we have seen, will leave an organisation long before their normal retirement date, whether through redundancy, early retirement or their own decision. We need therefore to consider a more comprehensive approach to helping them which can take account of all the different forms of transition.

Appraisal and older workers

A useful starting point is the employer's appraisal system. Although the form will vary, many organisations will have in place some form of systematic and regular appraisal of employees which looks back at past performance and forward at objectives and needs in the period ahead. The process may include personal development or training plans in which steps are agreed for meeting the combined needs of the business and the individual in the period ahead.

That is precisely the context within which the needs of the older employee can be most effectively addressed. A sound appraisal system which is respected and valued by everyone in the business can without any great difficulty be extended to include the particular questions which both employer and employee are likely to be concerned about during the final years of an individual's employment.

If preparation for the final period of work and for retirement is made in this way, it will become part of the employer's involvement in the development of the individual and is much less likely to be seen as an isolated and distinct process labelled 'pre-retirement education'.

Under such an arrangement, now often referred to as mid-life planning, there can be regular discussion between employer and individual employee not just on preparation for retirement, to which we shall return, but also on some of the vital issues relating to the remaining period of employment, for example:

- What are the options for the remaining period of employment? Should there be any changes in responsibility or in the place of work? Or in patterns of work? Is the employee concerned a potential trainer or counsellor?

- What are the individual's training requirements – whether related specifically to future tasks within the present or future job or to more general skills or to retirement?

- What is the most likely timing and manner of the individual's employment ending? Does he or she want to work right through to normal retirement age, if this is practicable?

- Is there an early retirement option? What are the terms?

- What is the best information the employer can provide on future staffing plans, including any reduction schemes? How are they likely to affect the individual?

- Are there any domestic or personal matters which the employee needs to bring to the employer's attention – for example any change in responsibilities for family and relations which may affect work? Any health issues? What help can the employer offer with these?

- What scope is there for the employee to become involved in external activities – for example voluntary work or educational programmes, whether in their own time or, if possible, in the employer's time? What support is the employer able to provide for these?

Policy decisions will be needed on how and when employees should be included in such focused appraisal arrangements. One option is to make such discussion an automatic part of appraisal for all employees over a defined age, say 45 or 50; or, bearing in mind the increasing number of employees leaving earlier, for all employees known to be within five or ten years of leaving.

The TOTAL case study on pages 105–106 provides an account of a major French company introducing arrangements very much along these lines as part of its normal appraisal system.

However it is done, the most important objective is to make sure that these issues are not left to guesswork, rumour and speculation but are automatically and regularly on the table as matters for discussion.

Some parts of such a discussion – particularly if the possibility of redundancy or early retirement becomes a reality – may not be easy. But if the arrangements apply to all employees at this stage of their careers and their options are reviewed as a matter of course, much of the anxiety and uncertainty can be eliminated.

Trade unions have an important role in supporting these processes and in thinking more widely about the special needs of their older members.

▪ Planning for retirement

The quality of retirement planning has improved significantly in recent years, notably through the work of the Pre-Retirement Association (PRA), whose advice underpins what follows.

One of the advantages of starting such preparation early – several years before retirement is due – is that aspects which cannot be left until the last minute, for example financial planning and health matters, can be addressed well in advance. Issues such as the use of time, opportunities for voluntary work and learning and the setting of personal objectives can then be tackled nearer the due date of retirement.

Retirement courses, whenever they are undertaken, need not and should not be didactic and authoritarian or undertaken simply in a classroom style. Some of the most effective programmes combine lectures and talks with work in groups and individual counselling.

The case study which follows includes Peugeot-Talbot's very successful use of professional actors to simulate some of the situations which people will face in retirement in order to help them think about the issues involved in advance and to plan accordingly.

Peugeot-Talbot Pre-retirement planning

Peugeot-Talbot encourages employees to keep the task of pension planning in mind by running a series of pre-retirement planning seminars – part of a wider programme entitled 'The Best of Times'.

At a one-day event aimed at 'mid-life planning', employees are taken through a guide book outlining the basics of planning in advance for retirement. The programme is currently offered to all employees aged 55 and over and their partners; the company intends to lower the age threshold to 50 and over in the next three years.

The seminar covers questions of lifestyle and health as well as financial and pension matters. An important and popular feature is the use of professional actors to present to participants some of the situations they will face in retirement. These sessions, although light-hearted, are nevertheless highly effective in helping employees to think about some of the issues they are likely to face.

The company runs a help service from an office in its main plant from which all employees are able to get advice and information on retirement issues.

A further seminar is offered to employees at 60 and over (the normal retirement age is 65) to discuss the specifics of pensions, as well as company and state benefits, tax and investment issues.

Peugeot also maintains contact with those who have been through the 'Best of Times' programme to get feedback and information to help improve it.

Several successful programmes have combined the use of external providers with the employer's own managers in running the programmes. (The Peugeot-Talbot system offers the best of both worlds by using the services of a consultant who was once employed by the company.)

Information on competent course providers is available from the PRA, as well as useful information and checklists on such matters as effective venues, cost, timing, advance preparation, involvement of spouses, size of courses and mix of participants – and an important reminder to make sure that financial advisers on these programmes are truly independent, and not there to sell a particular provider's wares.

Another tip from the PRA, which was confirmed in our discussions, was the value of providing a reasonable choice for participants in the subjects to be covered by a particular course. This avoids the impression that it is a passive process in which a mass of information is thrust at individuals, as distinct from an opportunity to discuss areas which the participants themselves have said will be of direct interest to them.

Employers have generally received good cooperation in arranging for outside organisations to be involved in courses – for example DSS Benefits Agency officials to talk about benefits and volunteer bureau staff to talk about opportunities for work in community organisations.

A retirement preparation programme is likely to be most effective if it is not just a one-off course but a package of different elements, spread over a period and including both individual advice and counselling and written information.

Another case study describes how Kingfisher reappraised and revised the retirement preparation it offered.

Kingfisher Preparation for retirement

(Kingfisher is the parent company of B&Q, whose experiences of completely staffing a store with older workers are described in an earlier case study.)

Kingfisher took some time to review practice by other employers against its own requirements. These were for:

- a cost-effective means of providing support and information in advance of retirement;

- a means of doing so for a highly dispersed business (Kingfisher has over 2,000 separate locations);

- ways of making the prospect and experience of retirement as informed and free from stress as possible;

- continuing to build their reputation as an employer which cares for its employees at all stages of their lives.

It soon decided that it did not favour the more traditional form of pre-retirement education, provided through courses arranged in the final two or three years before normal retirement. There were several reasons for this.

First, many people would find that they were receiving information too late to do anything about it – particularly in relation to improving their financial arrangements. Second, many of those in need of such support would have left the company by the time the course was arranged. (Kingfisher's normal retirement age is 60 but a significant number of employees leave the company before that age.) Third, it was not considered to be cost-effective to arrange across-the-board retirement courses for all employees.

Throughout its planning, Kingfisher has been determined to strike the right balance between achieving its objectives in supporting employees and doing so in a cost-effective manner, avoiding blanket solutions which do not necessarily provide the support where it is wanted.

Against this background, it concluded that it would introduce a policy in two parts.

The first of these involves a series of courses to provide information and help well in advance of retirement, when employees reach the age of 45. (They prefer to define eligibility by reference to an age rather than a number of years before retirement so that they can cover together employees who plan to stay until normal retirement age and those who opt to go early.)

The courses, for about 25 employees at a time and lasting for most of one day, are provided by an outside supplier and are predominantly financial in content. The company's view is that at this stage of their lives, employees are likely to be much more concerned with financial preparation than with questions about how they are going to use their time after retirement. Kingfisher accepts that there may in due course be a need to extend these courses to cover options for the period of employment remaining before retirement – although these may be equally well addressed separately in the appraisal process.

The courses include specialist speakers covering finance and investment issues and state pensions and benefits. Information is provided by the company's own pensions staff on the company's pension arrangements as they affect employees before, at and after retirement. There is also a short session on health issues.

These courses are initially being made available from manager level upwards, but the intention is to extend them in due course across more employees.

As the second part of its support, Kingfisher has decided to provide information to all employees two years before retirement in a different form – namely by means of audio tapes, coupled with a continuing helpline facility. (Audio was chosen rather than video because of the wider availability of audio equipment.)

These are provided by an outside supplier, customised for Kingfisher and updated yearly to ensure that they take account of external and internal changes. The tapes, together with a comprehensive booklet, provide a huge range of information geared to the much greater interest at that stage in post-retirement activities. They include, in a list of some 40 subjects, routes into voluntary work, adult education, moving house, making a will, fitness and exercise, and state pensions and benefits.

More detailed information and advice may be found in *Preparing for Retirement: The employer's guide*, written for the PRA and Age Concern England by Joanna Walker (see Publications from ACE Books). As the author puts it in her introduction, 'good preparation involves more than attendance on a course or a group of events, and requires a combination of stimuli to encourage people to think about their future in a constructive and positive way'.

▪ Involvement in community activities

More and more businesses are coming to accept that they have a responsibility as corporate citizens to play their part in the well-being of the communities on which they themselves depend for their trade and employment. Some have included in their offers of assistance to employees in preparation for retirement the opportunity to take part in their programmes for community involvement – opportunities which may be of particular interest and value to older employees. This may, for example, take the form of:

- helping employees who are interested in finding opportunities for voluntary work, probably in their own time but in some cases for limited periods of company time;

- offering employees opportunities for involvement in projects which are being supported by the employer;

- helping to arrange projects for groups of employee volunteers to undertake in their own time;

- providing matching financial support for the fundraising activities of employees;
- secondment of employees to community organisations, whether on a part-time or full-time basis.

The benefits to the employer include:

- feedback from volunteers about projects they are supporting – whether their funds are being well used and how the project concerned is progressing;
- the creation of valuable links between the business and the community which are not the result of purely financial contributions;
- the ability to offer employees opportunities for experience and fulfilment which it may not be possible to provide from within the organisation.

Other business benefits suggested in a useful paper by Action: Employees in the Community (now Business in the Community) include:

- the opportunity for positive public relations;
- the encouragement of new ways of thinking and fresh perspectives;
- the creation of new links with other companies and organisations.[2]

IBM provides an example of a company doing just this – and in a way suited to its own business.[3]

IBM The Volbase scheme

IBM has introduced a new scheme, known as Volbase, to match volunteers from within the company with voluntary groups that need them. This was done because of the large number of approaches that were made to the company for volunteer help and the problem of ringing round within the company to find the right person with the right skills at the right time. IBM's answer was to make the match through a database. The system involves an IBM location working with a volunteer broker agency, for example a volunteer bureau or a local office of Business in the Community.

IBM supplies the agency with the technology. The agency markets the matching service to local voluntary groups, and IBM offers it to its employees and retirees. Matching is just one keystroke away on the Volbase database.

In 1996, the service will be marketed to other companies, with all profits going to the broker agencies. More corporate subscribers could mean that voluntary bodies without the technology could be helped to get on-line and speedily access the service without a lot of form-filling.

Another report from Action: Employees in the Community sets out the benefits involved in supporting employees who serve on the boards of not-for-profit organisations, including charities, schools, health authorities, housing associations and enterprise agencies.[4]

For older employees in particular, arrangements of this sort provide an excellent means of sampling different forms of community activity in which they may wish to become more fully involved after retirement. Contacts are established for later development, dependence on work is tempered and the fear of the unknown in retirement is reduced.

▬ Employers and ex-employees

Not every organisation takes the view that once employees have left they can be forgotten and left to lead their own lives. Many who retire or who are made redundant will decide for themselves that they do not wish to have any further contact with their former employer. But for many, the offer of some form of contact may be very welcome, regarded both as courteous and as a recognition that they are not forgotten and that what they have contributed is not undervalued.

Continued contact may, for example, include making the company newspaper available to retired people, giving them access to company welfare and advice services, enabling them to take part in staff discount schemes and inviting them to functions. Pensioners may well have their own organisations for maintaining contact with each other, and a little support for these from the employer goes a long way.

A possible form of support which has great potential but which has not yet taken off in the UK on any large scale is exemplified in different ways by our next two case studies: BT's Skillbase in the Community scheme, later developed into Career Bridge, and the Travelers

Corporation scheme in the USA for using retired employees as sub-contractors. Both examples show how employer and ex-employees can derive mutual benefit from working together.

In the BT case, the company has been able to further its community objectives by making skilled resources available to community organisations free of charge while its employees have been given the opportunity to sample voluntary work after leaving employment.

BT Skillbase in the Community

Background

Over the last four years, BT has implemented a very large-scale reduction in its workforce through a series of Release programmes. As a result the numbers employed by BT have dropped from 215,000 in 1992 to the present level of 137,000.

The required reductions were achieved on a voluntary basis, through voluntary early retirement. In addition to compensation payments based on length of service and enhanced pension payments (paid immediately to those aged 50 and over), BT severance packages also included a number of options designed to help employees leaving the company to prepare for life after BT; these are described in a case study in Chapter 5 (p 110).

One of these options, which is the main topic of this case study, gives ex-employees the opportunity to work in a community organisation after leaving the company.

Skillbase in the Community

The initial BT Release programmes included the opportunity for managers and professional staff leaving the company to register with an independent company, Skillbase Ltd.

(Skillbase was founded in 1990 in conjunction with IBM to assist with that company's early retirement and voluntary redundancy schemes. Skillbase guaranteed part-time work for employees leaving IBM over a period of two years after separation. This enabled IBM to cope with quite severe reductions in staffing, yet to manage workload peaks, through retaining access to key skills through the transition period.

Through a combination of pension (where eligible), earnings from Skillbase and the yield from investing lump-sum payments, employees were able to enjoy a financial 'cushion' over the two-year period either to help the transition into retirement or to help them make a career change. It avoided the sudden culture shock of moving straight from employment one day to unemployment the next.

In addition to guaranteed work schemes, Skillbase also operates a Freelance Register. People with marketable skills may join this register at no cost to themselves, but with the possibility of work assignments with a variety of companies who are seeking skilled resources.

In early 1994 Skillbase was acquired by Hogg Robinson Financial Services.)

Registration of BT's ex-employees with Skillbase meant that the people concerned would leave the BT payroll on Release terms and would become employees of Skillbase. As such, they would be available to BT to work in the company for up to 60 days. They would be paid a daily rate based on their salary at the time of leaving and would be guaranteed the 60 days' payment whether or not BT called on their services. A similar scheme for non-managerial employees was operated with Manpower plc.

A total of just under 3,000 people registered with Skillbase. However, it soon became clear that BT could not make use within its own work requirements of all the capacity available on the Skillbase register. This meant that some individuals who had been willing and anxious to work for up to 60 days were not getting the opportunity to do so (although they were getting the payment) and that the company was getting no return from its payment to these individuals.

Accordingly BT decided to widen the scope of the Skillbase scheme so that the services of some of those who had registered could, if the individuals concerned were interested, be offered to community organisations, free of any charge to them. The Skillbase in the Community scheme was established in 1993; it was initially run by Skillbase but

later separated. The scheme had the following features:

- Individuals still on the register were asked whether they would be interested in using some or all of the 60 days in working for a community organisation.

- A list was prepared of voluntary organisations with whom BT had links, both nationally and locally, through its community programme.

- Organisations on this list were approached; not surprisingly, all of them indicated that they would be interested in taking part in the scheme.

- The organisations were asked to specify what jobs needed doing, what skills and experience were required, and where.

- BT established a system, using ex-employees registered with Skillbase, for matching the organisations' requests with available and suitable individuals.

- Assignments were agreed individually, ranging from a few days to the full 60 days, some full-time, some part-time.

- In matching the requirements, account was taken of the likelihood of individuals, especially older employees, being able to form more permanent links with the organisations for whom they would be working.

- The organisations were asked to supply a report at the end of the assignment to help BT in operating the scheme.

Skillbase in the Community worked well. A total of 199 assignments were agreed. They included, for example, installation of computer systems, setting up helplines, public relations, accounting and personnel tasks, organising conferences, surveys and market research, fundraising, implementation of quality systems, organisation of competitions and anniversary projects, and reviews of internal organisation and procedures.

Among the benefits to BT were:

- the ability to use as a positive feature of the company's community programme a resource which would otherwise be wasted;

- a widening of the nature of company support for community organisations beyond the more familiar financial donations;

- fulfilment of its wish to support individuals in making the transition from BT employment.

The scheme enabled individuals to:

- continue to earn some income for a period beyond the end of BT employment;

- gain experience of working in a voluntary organisation without a permanent commitment;

- obtain an introduction that might lead to more permanent involvement in the voluntary sector.

For the community organisations, the scheme provided:

- access to skills free of charge which they might have found it difficult or expensive to obtain by other means;

- the flexibility to have specific tasks undertaken without permanent increases in their staffing.

Several of the organisations expressed surprise at the high level of skill, training and commitment which the people concerned brought with them, which were taken for granted within BT as a result of normal training and experience.

In a survey of participating organisations at the end of the first year of the scheme:

- 99 per cent were satisfied with the way in which the project was carried out;

- 41 per cent said that the person concerned would be staying on with the organisation in some capacity;

- 100 per cent said that they would be interested in taking part in similar schemes in the future ('You bet!' 'Yes! How soon can I apply?').

Not surprisingly, some problems were also encountered. Some mismatches did occur, with overqualified individuals being supplied in some cases, and difficulties were experienced in completing some projects within the agreed timescales.

The overwhelming response was, however, very positive:

- 'Ex-BT managers have a great deal to offer the voluntary sector.'

- 'The limited resources of our organisation were a culture shock to the secondee, but the project was carried out in a very professional manner.'

- 'The secondee was extremely well organised and prepared a structured plan which we were able to use even after he had left.'

Career Bridge

Following the success of Skillbase in the Community, BT has decided to retain a similar scheme in its remaining Release programmes, but in a slightly different form. The scheme is now run on behalf of BT by Manpower plc. The guarantee is now for 40 days' work rather than 60 days'; the package includes a cash payment which may be used for training or to provide extra financial help prior to starting a new job and also the opportunity to attend a course in basic computer literacy skills.

The scheme remains popular with both individuals and community organisations.

Replication elsewhere of schemes like Skillbase in the Community and Career Bridge could lead to a massive injection of resources into the voluntary sector as well as helping employers to manage transitions from work by providing a direct benefit to employees.

The Travelers case study, from the USA, describes the use of a flexible corps of ex-employees who are familiar with the business instead of hiring unknown and untried external temporary staff for dealing with peaks and troughs in the employer's labour requirements.[5]

The Travelers Corporation Retiree Job Bank

In the late 1970s, the Travelers started a customer service hotline and needed employees who were familiar with company operations and procedures to staff it. Removing full-time employees from their departments for this purpose would have disrupted the company's normal operations, so the Travelers decided to hire back some of its retirees.

Because the company's pension plan restricted the number of hours that retirees could work, they were hired on a part-time basis. The Travelers had no trouble recruiting retirees at a reasonable cost, and customers found the hotline staff to be patient and knowledgeable.

The success of the hotline encouraged the Travelers to consider using its retirees in other roles. When a 1980 survey of older employees revealed that many were interested in continuing to work past retirement, the Travelers recognised an ideal opportunity simultaneously to reduce its high temporary agency costs, to gain an on-call staff that was familiar with the company and had a known performance record, and to offer employees the prospect of an even longer-term relationship with the company, which could ease the transition to retirement. In 1981 the Travelers Retiree Job Bank was established.

The job bank was set up in a centralised office where retirees registered and all requests from company managers for temporary help were processed. When employees retired, they were given the opportunity to register with the job bank. The Travelers found that it had little need to recruit formally for this programme because of the number of retirees who opted to register.

Wages were negotiated on an individual basis, according to each employee's qualifications. The wage structure was tailored to benefit both the employees and the company. From the retirees' point of view, the wage rates offered by the Travelers were generally more comparable to their pre-retirement salaries than the wages offered by independent agencies. For its part, the Travelers was able to avoid paying agency commissions and did not offer benefits because retirees received substantial health benefits as part of their pension plan.

Retirees were classified according to their qualifications, preferred job types and availability for work. A personnel file was kept on each retiree. When a department needed temporaries for jobs ranging from envelope stuffing to complicated computer programming and managerial tasks, it called the job bank office.

Often, the department requested one of its own retirees to return to his or her former position, in order to fill in for a co-worker on leave or to solve a special problem requiring the retiree's experience. If a suitable retiree was not available, the job bank office forwarded the request to an outside agency.

Departmental managers responded enthusiastically to the programme. By 1985 the demand for retiree temps was more than double the supply, and the Travelers

decided to expand the bank to include retirees from other insurance firms. Because this meant more formal recruiting, the Travelers began a number of publicity campaigns, including holding an 'un-retirement party' to recruit the retirees of other firms in the Hartford area and encouraging Travelers retirees to enlist their friends.

The non-Travelers retirees were processed in much the same way as the Travelers retirees, but needed an initiation period to learn about the company. During this period, they were not at peak productivity, but they proved to be reliable and motivated, and soon performed at the levels of the Travelers retirees. Because most of these retirees already had health benefits, no additional benefits were offered.

By January 1990, the demand for temporary workers had expanded to the point where the Travelers embarked on another new undertaking. It formed its own in-house temporary agency called TravTemps to replace the outside agencies from which it used to hire temporaries. TravTemps enlarged the company's pool of temporary labour to include both retirees and younger workers. Once the new workers were recruited, their assignment and use paralleled those of retiree temps.

In addition to forming TravTemps, with its new recruiting strategy, the company made two modifications to the job bank at this time. First, the programme began to offer a benefits package to its workers: temporary employees who worked over 500 hours in a six-month period became eligible for holiday pay and modest health insurance benefits. This allowed the Travelers to attract people who might otherwise have joined other temporary placement firms in the area. Second, the programme standardised its wage-setting strategy. Formerly, the wages of temporary workers had been set according to individual qualifications, regardless of the job assignment. Under the new system, pay was determined by actual job requirements.

Today over 400 temporaries (250 of whom are Travelers retirees) work for the company in any given week, meeting over 90 per cent of all departmental requests. The remainder of these positions are filled by outside agencies. The average age of retiree temps is 67, and nearly 70 per cent are women. Non-retirees tend to be much younger, averaging about 33 years of age. Retirees work an average of 516 hours per year and are most likely to work in unskilled production. Non-retirees work an average of 608 hours per year, most often as secretaries. The only workers that TravTemps places in technical and skilled production positions are former Travelers employees because these jobs tend to require specific company experience.

The difference in cost between using temporaries from the retiree job bank and using outside agencies can be estimated by comparing what it actually cost the Travelers to operate the job bank with an estimate of what it would have cost to fill the same positions with outside agency temporaries. In 1989 the Travelers paid a total of $2.05 million for job bank temporaries. If it had hired independent

agency temporaries instead, it would have spent $3.08 million (calculated by multiplying the hours actually worked by retirees by the price charged per hour by an independent agency).

By setting up the job bank, the Travelers thus reduced its labour costs by $1.03 million in 1989, or an average of $4.88 per job bank employee hour. These labour savings were offset somewhat by the cost of operating the job bank ($157,000), yielding net job bank savings of over $870,000.

Travelers managers, finding retirees reliable and motivated, have reported high levels of satisfaction with the retiree job bank. One job bank staff member recalls a blinding Hartford snowstorm when few regular employees showed up for work but nearly every retiree was at work on time. This commendable reliability can be compared to that of agency temporaries, who have an absenteeism rate of up to 15 per cent.

Operating the job bank 'in-house' allows the Travelers ultimate control over the temporaries it hires. Through the job bank, the company has the flexibility needed to hire the retiree most suited to the requirements of a specific job. And by hiring retirees with a long-standing relationship with the company, the Travelers makes sure it already has reliable information on their work performance. This in turn reduces the risks that many companies face in hiring temporaries whose skills and performance are unknown.

The Travelers' experience with its retiree job bank has been a highly positive one. It has boosted the morale of full-time employees, who view the company as 'taking care of its own'. The scheme has saved the company over 25 per cent of the cost of hiring temporaries from outside agencies, and it has achieved equally important, but less tangible, rewards such as improved productivity and better employee relations.

A few UK employers have decided to provide support for retirees who wish to become involved in voluntary work. This not only helps to reduce the impression which people who retire may easily gain that, once they are retired, they are forgotten, but also helps meet the responsibility of the employer to provide support for people at all stages of their association with an organisation.

Marks and Spencer Retiree volunteering

This, for example, is the objective of Marks and Spencer in their support for retiree volunteering. This is undertaken by giving support to retired staff who are prepared to act as focal points for other company retirees who may wish to do voluntary work but do not have the necessary information and contacts. Working through the company's Retired Staff Associations, these individuals are supported by the company in providing links between potential volunteers and local volunteer organisations and charities.

Similarly Whitbread, a pioneer of employee volunteering in the UK, encourages its retirees to form links with the company's numerous employee volunteer committees throughout the country. In this way, Whitbread is able to offer support and recognition for retiree volunteers, building on the work of the Whitbread Retirement Association.

Both employee and retiree volunteering arrangements have an important role in increasing the availability of volunteer resources. As already mentioned, one of the more surprising findings of the Carnegie Inquiry into the Third Age was that, in spite of the extra time which retired people are likely to have in their lives, the proportion of retirees who become involved in voluntary work is actually smaller than the proportion of younger age groups still at work.

The reasons are not easy to understand; they may relate partly to another form of age discrimination, in which older people are discouraged from volunteering by various forms of age limits within charities. However, the same evidence also showed that, once older people become involved as volunteers, they tend to stay involved and to offer greater amounts of time. It follows that schemes such as these are an excellent way of tapping into this much-needed source of support and maintaining it on a durable basis.

Our final case study describes the work of REACH, which specialises in recruiting retired or redundant professional and managerial employees and placing them as part-time volunteers with local voluntary organisations in need of their individual experience.

REACH Volunteering opportunities

One way in which employers can help those who are making the transition from work – whether this is through redundancy or retirement, early or normal – is by bringing to their attention opportunities to use in the voluntary sector the skills and experience that they have gained at work. This is not, however, an easy task for the individual company to undertake itself, particularly where the employee has business or professional expertise. The services of REACH are tailor-made for this purpose.

The task is an important one: voluntary organisations are always in need of specific skills, whether on a permanent or a temporary basis, and experience has shown that, with a good matching of opportunities and a will on the part of both parties to learn about each other's worlds, people from industry and commerce and from voluntary organisations have a great deal to offer each other.

For the individual, the opportunity to work in the voluntary sector may be an important element of building a new and fulfilling life after the end of full-time paid work.

REACH and how it works

REACH was established as a registered charity in 1979. Its task is to find part-time, expenses-only jobs for retired or redundant business or other professional men and women who want to use their maturity, experience and skills to help charities. The services of REACH are provided free of charge to both the individuals and the charities which it serves.

Individuals with professional or business skills tell REACH by means of a simple form about their experience, expertise and interests, as well as where they want to work, when and for how long. Most REACH volunteers work for one or two days a week, but sometimes assignments are arranged as short or longer-term projects or to suit varied patterns of availability on the part of the individual.

In parallel, REACH maintains a register of jobs which charities want filled. Thousands of UK charities, large and small, national and local, are regular customers of REACH.

The two sets of requirements are then brought together by a team of experienced 'matchers'. The matchers are all volunteers and retired professional people themselves.

The individual is sent details of possible jobs to consider. Once a choice is made, the individual is introduced to the charity so that details can be discussed and both parties can make sure that the chemistry is right. Once the introduction is over and the assignment is agreed, REACH withdraws and the parties take it from there – although there are many repeat customers.

REACH also runs a network of Coordinators, so that people who are thinking about volunteering can talk it through with an experienced volunteer in their own area.

REACH works closely with professional bodies and outplacement agencies.

All the jobs which are handled are done without salary – with expenses only being paid to the individual by the charity.

Most charities are positive about offering older people the opportunity to contribute without age barriers and discrimination. REACH has, however, taken a strong stand against any discrimination by charities on grounds of age and will not handle an assignment for any organisation which operates arbitrary age limits for its volunteers.

Some 750 individual jobs were arranged in 1995 and the number of placements is growing each year.

Operating costs are kept to a minimum. REACH itself is largely staffed by volunteers working alongside the four permanent paid staff.

Some funds are provided by Government and trusts but the bulk of the income comes from the many employers who have come to value the service over many years.

Employers and REACH

The provision of information to employees about the services of REACH is a natural and valuable part of the service which a good employer will provide to those who are leaving employment – whether through redundancy or retirement.

Information about REACH's service is regularly provided through channels such as in-house newsletters and company pre-retirement courses. Straightforward information leaflets about the service (available from REACH) are an essential part of a package of information for people about to retire or receiving advice and support in a redundancy programme.

People acting as counsellors for employers, whether as employees or subcontractors, regularly find that providing information about REACH is an important and useful part of their role. It is seen by existing employees as a positive means of supporting those who are leaving.

Voluntary organisations

The organisations that have used REACH for years speak highly of its service – efficiently and economically undertaken by experienced people. The idea of finding a REACH volunteer for a task does not always immediately occur to a charity manager but those who have used it have come to value the quality of the placement – and of course the free resource that is provided.

In 1995 REACH broadened its activities to offer advice to organisations thinking of using volunteers with a business or professional background but needing help in sorting out their needs and how they can best be met.

Related organisations

REACH's activities are complementary to those offered by volunteer bureaux and other organisations. It believes strongly in working in partnership and does not compete with others for its focused skill-based placement service.

- **RSVP** (Retired and Senior Volunteer Programme), mainly concerned with setting up projects in which groups of older volunteers with a variety of skills and experience come together to carry out specific tasks for the benefit of the local community;

- **BESO** (British Executive Service Overseas), which sets up short-term advisory or training projects in developing countries for qualified specialist volunteers;

- **NAVB** (National Association of Volunteer Bureaux), the umbrella organisation for the 300 or so volunteer bureaux which operate in many parts of Britain arranging voluntary jobs for anyone – young, old, skilled or not – with local charities.

Examples

A few cases of recent voluntary job placements will illustrate the scope and diversity of the REACH matching service.

- **John McHale of Epsom in Surrey** had a hands-on managerial career in transport, distribution and fleet management, including operational and cost responsibility for 1,500 commercial vehicles and cars. After his retirement, REACH found him a voluntary appointment as logistics consultant with the environmental charity, **Bioregional Development Group**. His job is to help with an imaginative project to revive woodlands coppicing to make locally produced charcoal for distribution as barbecue fuel through a major DIY chain.

- **Benny Field**'s career as a senior secretary and PA made her the ideal candidate to work as a volunteer in the Action for Blind People's regional fundraising office, based in the charity's Weston-super-Mare holiday hotel. Benny spends one day a week on office duties and another day helping with the running of a day centre – 'enjoying the company of 20 delightful ladies!'

- **Dr Nabil Mobarak** was well qualified to join **NCH Action for Children** after a distinguished career as a senior consultant paediatrician. Nabil is working as project volunteer on one of the charity's many initiatives to bring a better quality of life to Britain's most vulnerable children and young people: the Independent Representation and Complaints Service, based at Maidstone in Kent.

- **Duncan Dingsdale**, an ex-paratrooper and former chief press photographer of the *Glasgow Herald*, may find life slightly less hectic since his retirement, but his REACH voluntary jobs still keep him pretty busy. He is already a case worker with the East Lothian branch of **SSAFA** (the Soldiers, Sailors and Air Force Association) and is joining **Age Concern** in Edinburgh as information officer.

- **Stuart Aldridge** of Solihull was the Managing Director of an engineering consultancy which he led from loss into substantial profit in just two years. Stuart's business experience is now being used in a different way to help with the development in the Midlands of the **Princess Royal Trust for Carers**. This charity was set up five years ago to provide centres throughout the country where people who care for others who are sick or disabled can go for practical advice, counselling and support. Says Stuart, 'I am very happy to be putting something back into the community in an area where my business experience is of value.'

The average age of REACH volunteers has been falling over the years and is now just under 60. However, jobs are still being found for people in their 60s, 70s and even 80s, demonstrating just how little age has got to do with ability.

Employers' action points

- How important to you is it to support employees in making the transition from work to retirement or life after redundancy?

- Have you considered how this can enhance the reputation of the business as a good employer and improve the performance and productivity of employees in the final period of work?

- At what stage do you think that you should start providing this support?

- What do you think are employees' greatest needs at this stage of their careers?
  To prepare for retirement?
  To feel less uncertainty about their remaining years of employment?
  To be esteemed within the business?
  To be listened to, make a contribution and feel wanted?

- Do you run any form of pre-retirement programme?

- Do you offer employees a choice as to what subjects it should cover?

- Do you provide an opportunity for spouses to be involved?
- Do you provide pre-retirement information and support other than courses?
- Have you considered helping to find opportunities for voluntary work for your existing employees? Or for people who have retired from your organisation? How might this link with your organisation's activities in the community?
- What support and contact do you maintain with people who have retired from your organisation?
- Have you considered using retired employees who are interested in working as subcontractors for your business?

7 Conclusion

Employers should not underestimate the benefits which can flow from tackling the various issues we have addressed.

The successful businesses of the future are going to be those which are not only leaner and fitter, or even leaner and better, but able to find ways of becoming distinctive and outstanding in their markets.

In so doing, a key test will be how well they use the intelligence, skills and experience of all their employees. Success will not be generated simply through decisions in boardrooms and top-down strategies. It will depend just as much on whether the leaders of organisations listen to employees, use their collective intellects and expertise and involve them in designing success.

The alternative is to assume that all wisdom lies at the top and in the centre; to regard employees simply as those affected by decisions, instead of inviting them to share in making and owning the decisions; to see them merely as another item of cost, to be reduced to the absolute minimum – to be bought, stored, used or disposed of as a commodity.

These are critical issues for the UK as a nation as we compete with economies which are ahead of us in taking a long-term view of industrial investment. We have in this country a financial system which puts enormous short-term pressures on businesses to provide high early returns to investors, most of whom have only an arms-length and often temporary stake in our companies. The average shareholding by big institutional investors in Britain is held for only four years – in what Handy describes as a discardable responsibility.[1] As a result, there is a dangerous pressure on employers to respond to shareholders' needs by taking a similarly short-term view of employment – and particularly by sacrificing continuity and expertise to cost-cutting.

Perhaps some of our businesses will move in time to new forms of ownership and investment – for example on the model of the successful John Lewis Partnership – in which the idea that a business exists for the good of all is self-evident and potent.

In the meantime, even under the prevailing forms of ownership, there is a powerful case for looking beyond tomorrow's share price at the longer-term employment issues which we have viewed through the eyes of older employees. If shareholders are not pressing these issues today, they may well have cause in the medium term for thanking those directors and company leaders who had the vision to do so.

We hope that the promise made in the opening chapter has been fulfilled – that this book has not been about special pleading for older people. If it had been, we doubt whether the employers who have participated would have shown the degree of interest and cooperation which has been at the heart of this project.

They have recognised that this issue is a part of the management of people which has been neglected and which has the potential, if that continues, to do serious damage – and, if addressed, to yield significant benefit.

The employers who can work through the five checklists in this book and commit their businesses to action in the areas suggested may in time be surprised at the combined impact of a programme of action on all those fronts.

Such a programme will, we believe, provide:

- new opportunities for making the best use of the special qualities of older employees and the investment that they represent;

- a means of responding to possible future skill shortages;

- a widening of the pool of available talent and an important insight into the demographic factors which will so strongly influence both the labour market and the customer base of the next century;

- the opportunity to make improvements in employment practice which will benefit not just older workers but all employees;

- an awakening to the waste and folly of age discrimination;

- a fresh view on approaches to reducing manpower;
- a new look at the importance of a diverse and well-balanced workforce and a counter to the threat of a disillusioned and wasted element in the workforce;
- an opportunity to help build the reputation of a business as a caring and thoughtful employer, looking after the needs of all its employees.

NOTES

1 Introduction – New lives in a new century

1 Dominique Balmary, French Government representative, speaking at a conference in Nice, June 1995.

2 Employment and age

1 These headings are based on the work of Professor Alan Walker of Sheffield University and Dr Philip Taylor of the Policy Studies Institute.

2 Charles Handy, *The Empty Raincoat*.

3 Dr David Parsons, *Defusing the Demographic Time Bomb*.

4 Motoko Rich, 'The bomb that didn't go off', *Financial Times*, 17 February 1995.

5 Forecasts and estimates from *Social Trends 1995* and Labour Force Surveys (HMSO).

6 Ibid.

7 Survey by the Business and Technology Education Council, August 1995.

8 But not exclusively in the retail industry. Britannia Life was reported (*Scotsman*, 6 May 1994) as having decided to take on 200 people aged 40 and over, based on their ability and positive attitude and the company's need for a more balanced age profile.

9 Rodney Buse, Group Personnel Director, W H Smith, speaking at Age Concern conference on employment and age, Gresham College, May 1995.

10 *World Labour Report 1995*.

11 See, for example, John Atkinson and N Meager, *New Forms of Work Organisation*; Charles Handy, *The Age of Unreason*, Chapter 4.

12 *Social Trends 1995* and Labour Force Surveys.

13 Will Hutton, *The State We're In*.

14 Roger Lyons, General Secretary of MSF, speech in 1995.

15 Handy, *The Age of Unreason*, Chapter 7.

16 Tom Peters, *Liberation Management*.

17 Chris Brewster et al, *Flexible Working Patterns in Europe*.

18 Department of Employment, *A Manager's Guide to Teleworking*.

19 Brewster, *Flexible Working Patterns in Europe*.

3 The needs of older workers

1 Speech by Rodney Buse, Group Personnel Director, W H Smith, at the Industrial Society, June 1994.

2 This is the system used by Marks and Spencer for dealing with pensions for those transferring to part-time work.

3 Genevieve Reday-Mulvey of the Geneva Association, writing in *Ageing International*, Washington DC, July 1995.

4 US Department of Labor, *Labor Market Problems of Older Workers*.

5 Trinder et al, *Employment: The role of work in the Third Age*.

6 Tom Schuller and Anne Marie Bostyn, *Education, Training and Information in the Third Age*.

7 S Downs and A Clark, *Training Requirements of the Older Worker*.

8 Metropolitan Recruitment Agency (METRA), *Lifting the Age Barrier: A practical guide*.

9 Robert Anderson, *Training Developments and Needs of Older Workers*.

10 Marc Thompson, *Last in the Queue?*

11 This case study is based on an article which first appeared in the February 1995 edition of *Prospects*, a quarterly magazine for the over-50s produced by the Scottish Community Education Council (SCEC) and the *Herald* newspaper. It is reproduced by kind permission of SCEC and Kvaerner-Govan Ltd.

12 Institute of Personnel Management, *Age and Employment*.

13 Ibid.

14 David Grayson of Business in the Community, speaking at an Age Concern conference on age and employment at Gresham College, May 1995.

15 Crossroads, *Looking Forward to Looking After*.

16 Carers in Employment Group, *Carers in Employment*.

17 Ibid.

18 Sylviane Sechaud, Ministry of Labour, France, speaking at a conference in Nice, June 1995.

4   Age and Equal Opportunities

1   The Sex Discrimination Act 1975 and the Race Relations Act 1976.

2   Figures from Opportunity 2000.

3   Ann McGoldrick, *The Employment of Older Workers in the 1990s*.

4   Maura Lantrua and Roy Jones, *Study of Age Restrictions on Employment Service Vacancies*.

5   Results of a Gallup poll, 1994.

6   Carnegie UK Trust, *Report of the Carnegie Inquiry*.

7   Results of a 1993 Eurobarometer survey quoted by Alan Walker in *Investing in Ageing Workers*.

8   Peter Naylor, *Age No Barrier*.

9   Survey by Sanders and Sidney, November 1995.

10   Research for the Carnegie Inquiry into the Third Age, 1993.

11   *Walker, Nolan and Kiddy* v *Carbodies Ltd*, Coventry, May 1994 – Industrial Tribunal, Birmingham.

12 Institute of Personnel Management, *Age and Employment*.

13 McGoldrick, *The Employment of Older Workers*.

14 House of Commons Employment Committee, 1989.

15 Marc Thompson, *Last in the queue?*

16 *World Labour Report 1995.*

17 *Population Projections 1962-2062.*

18 Carnegie UK Trust, *Report of the Carnegie Inquiry*.

19 *Walker, Nolan and Kiddy* v *Carbodies Ltd* (see note 10).

20 Parliamentary Answers (Hansard), 1994

21 The Labour Party, *Charter for Employees*.

22 US Congress, *Developments in Ageing*.

23 D O'Meara, *Protecting the Growing Number of Older Workers*.

24 Moore et al, *An International Overview of Employment Policies and Practices towards Older Workers.*

25 Research among employers by Philip Taylor and Alan Walker, University of Sheffield, in 1991, reported in the *Employment Gazette*, Department of Employment.

26 Survey by Institute of Management, 1995.

27 British Gas representative at Institute of Personnel Management conference, 1994.

28 Report of the Commission on Social Justice, p 196.

29 Institute of Personnel Management *Statement on Age and Employment*.

30 TUC, *Age Discrimination – Guidance for trade unions*.

5 Workforce reduction and older workers

1 Survey by MSF on early retirement, 1995.

2 *The Times*, 5 January 1995.

3 D J Berry-Lound, *Is Retirement Working?*

4 *Allsop* v *North Tyneside Metropolitan Borough Council*, Court of Appeal, March 1992.

5 *The Money Programme*, 1994.

6 Case study based on presentation to conference in Nice, June 1995, by M Pierre Proust of TOTAL.

7 *The Times*, 5 April 1995.

8 Report of the Commission on Social Justice, p 193.

9 Philip Taylor and Alan Walker, *Utilising Older Workers*.

6 The transition to retirement

1 Handy, *The Empty Raincoat*, p 137.

2 Action: Employees in the Community, *The Business Case*.

3 Based on an article in *NCVO News*, February 1995.

4 Action: Employees in the Community, *Business on Board*.

5 This case study from the USA is based on a background paper prepared by William McNaught and Michael C Barth for the Commonwealth Fund.

7 Conclusion

1 Handy, *The Empty Raincoat*, p 149.

APPENDIX 1: LIST OF PARTICIPATING ORGANISATIONS

The following 39 organisations contributed to the project through a combination of discussion, suggestion, participation in surveys, comments on the text and provision of material:

Employers

B&Q plc

Bank of England

British Airways

BT plc

City of Bradford Metropolitan Council

Glaxo Group Research and Development Ltd

IBM

Kingfisher plc

Kvaerner-Govan Ltd

Manpower plc

Marks and Spencer plc

Midland Bank plc

National Westminster Bank plc

Peugeot-Talbot Motor Co plc

Post Office

TSB

W H Smith

Other organisations

Age Concern England

Business in the Community

Confederation of British Industry

Department for Education and Employment

European Foundation for the Improvement of Living and Working Conditions

Health Education Authority

Help the Aged

Host Consultancy

Industrial Society

Institute of Employment Studies

Institute of Management

Institute of Personnel and
Development

Manchester Metropolitan
University, Department of
Management

Metropolitan Recruitment
Agency (METRA)

MSF

Policy Studies Institute

Pre-Retirement Association

Princess Royal Trust for Carers

Public Finance Foundation

REACH

Third Age Challenge Trust

University of Sheffield,
Department of Sociological
Studies

APPENDIX 2: LEAVING EMPLOYMENT EARLY – SURVEY OF EARLY RETIREES

A postal survey was conducted by the Institute for Employment Studies (IES) in September and October of 1995 of people who had retired before the normal retirement age during the previous five years from seven employing organisations. Questionnaires were sent to 1,698 people and completed responses were received from 1,010, a response rate of 60 per cent.

The aim of the survey was to explore the views and subsequent experiences of a group of people who had taken early retirement, whether through their own choice or not. This appendix provides only a brief summary of some of the findings. A full report will be published by the Institute for Employment Studies in 1996.

Reason for leaving

Of those responding to the survey:

- 70 per cent said that they took early retirement.

- 24 per cent felt that they were made redundant.

- 6 per cent said that it was a combination of the two or described it in some other way.

Over half of those who replied felt that leaving the organisation was fully their choice, while a third felt that they had some choice (they could have stayed but did not like the options on offer). Fifteen per cent reported that they had no choice about whether to leave or not.

The majority of people participating in the study left their job during a major programme of early retirement and/or redundancy being carried out by their employer. The survey shows that they had very mixed feelings about leaving.

Thirteen per cent said that they left for health reasons. In a few cases this appeared to be because of the nature of the work, for example it was outdoor and/or physically demanding. Stress had also played a part. However, the majority were experiencing conditions which affect many people as they age.

Just over a quarter said that they had taken advantage of the opportunity to leave as they were unhappy with changes occurring in the organisation. It was said, for example, that work was no longer enjoyable and that managers were driven by values which no longer acted to the benefit of employee or customer.

Eighteen per cent reported leaving work because their job had gone and the alternatives were not attractive. Some jobs had disappeared altogether; others were being relocated and respondents did not want to move at that point in their life or commute long distances.

Almost a third said that they had accepted the package they were offered, being pleased to take up new opportunities or have the time to pursue their own interests.

Looking for other jobs

Taking early retirement/redundancy did not mean that all respondents saw their working lives as over. Two-fifths reported that they did not want another job at the point when they left work. By the time of the survey, this number had risen to 45 per cent. Although the youngest respondents were in their early 50s, a significant minority were approaching retirement age and did see their working life as over.

Just over a quarter of respondents said that finding another job had been important to them immediately on leaving their employer. This proportion had risen slightly by the time of the survey. The increase may be accounted for by several factors. Some respondents, for example, had taken advantage of the free time to go on holidays or catch up with domestic responsibilities before thinking of the longer term. Others had begun to realise the financial implications of not having a job.

Almost half the sample had looked for another job (full- or part-time). Almost a quarter of these had had a job lined up for when they left. Some had taken a year or more to find a job, some were still looking and some had given up (see Figure 1).

Figure 1 Length of time taken to find another job (based on the 47 per cent who had looked for another job)

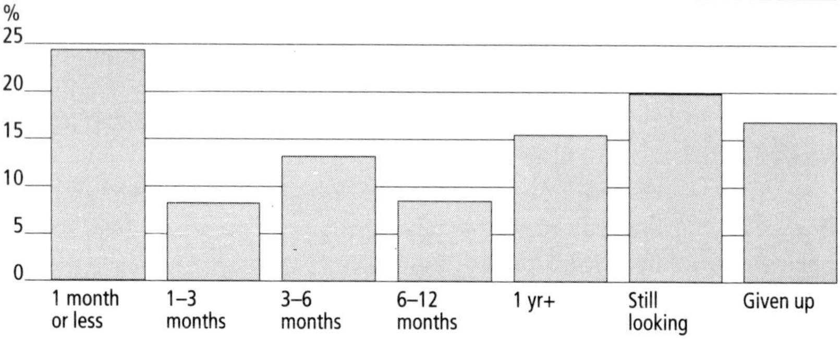

Over half of those who had looked for a job reported that they had found it fairly or very difficult to find one.

Competition for jobs and a lack of mobility were seen as major factors affecting people's success in finding a job. Two-thirds felt that employers preferred to recruit younger people and that this had had or was having a major effect on their success. Almost half felt that there were too many people looking for jobs in their area of the country. The majority did not feel that their skills and qualifications were out of date, although a third did say that this might be having a slight effect on the success of their job search.

Financial position

Almost all respondents left their job with some sort of financial package. Two-fifths reported that they were slightly less well off immediately on leaving their job compared to just before and a third that they were very much less well off. Although the majority reported feeling very or fairly secure financially when they left, a minority (around a tenth) did not feel at all secure.

By the time of the survey, a slightly higher proportion of respondents felt that they were less well off than before they left their job. It must be remembered that respondents had left their jobs at various times over the past few years, and the length of time they had been in this position may have affected their financial situation.

Apart from the company pension, the most frequently mentioned source of income was 'income from savings/investment'. Just over 60 per cent of respondents said that this was a source of income. Another small group were largely reliant on state benefits.

The provision of support and advice

Two-thirds of respondents said that they had received some advice and/or support on adjusting to their changed circumstances from the organisation they were leaving. The majority felt that this advice had been good. However, almost a third reported that it was 'reasonable' and 8 per cent that it was poor.

A third described other types of support and advice they would have liked to receive, including more concrete advice about the realities of managing with a reduced income, and about the state benefit system. Some respondents also said that the advice was given too late, or too near to the time they actually left work.

APPENDIX 3: USEFUL ADDRESSES

Age Concern
See page 154 for addresses of the national organisations.

Business in the Community
Promotes corporate and employee community involvement.

8 Stratton Street
London W1X 5FD
Tel: 0171-629 2209

British Executive Service Overseas (BESO)
Arranges advisory or training projects in developing countries for qualified specialist volunteers.

164 Vauxhall Bridge Road
London SW1V 2RA
Tel: 0171-630 0644

Carers in Employment Group
Alliance of organisations concerned for the welfare of working carers.

c/o Princess Royal Trust for Carers
16 Byward Street
London EC3R 5BA
Tel: O171-480 7788

Carnegie Third Age Programme
Follow-up programme to the Carnegie Inquiry into the Third Age.

3 Robert Street
London WC2N 6BH
Tel: 0171-976 1785

Department for Education and Employment
For information on 'Getting On' campaign and Advisory Group on Older Workers.

Caxton House
Tothill Street
London SW1H 9NF
Tel: 0171-273 6969
(public enquiries)

Help the Aged
Works to improve the quality of life
of elderly people.

St James's Walk
Clerkenwell Green
London ECIR OBE
Tel: 0171-253 0253

Institute of Management
Broad-based management institute,
providing research on management topics,
including attitudes to ageism.

2 Savoy Court
Strand
London WC2R 0EZ
Tel: 0171-497 0580

Institute of Personnel and Development
(formerly the Institute of Personnel
Management)
The professional body for human
resources and personnel managers.

IPD House
Camp Road
Wimbledon
London SW19 4UX
Tel: 0181-946 9100

Metropolitan Recruitment Agency
(METRA)
Consortium of local authorities sharing
a common interest in promoting best
practice in recruitment and retention
activities.

PO Box 1540
Homer Road
Solihull
West Midlands B91 3QB
Tel: 0121-704 6699

National Association of Volunteer
Bureaux (NAVB)
Umbrella organisation for the volunteer
bureaux which arrange voluntary jobs
throughout Britain.

St Peter's College
College Road
Saltley
Birmingham B8 3TE
Tel: 0121-327 0265

POPE (People of Previous Experience)
Employment assistance for older people
in the Bradford area.

William Morrison
Enterprise Trust
Enterprise 5
Five Lane Ends
Bradford BD10 8EW
Tel: 01274 614949

Pre-Retirement Association
Provides training, information and support for mid-life and retirement planning.

Nodus Centre
University Campus
Guildford
Surrey GUT 5RX
Tel: 01483 259747

REACH
Finds voluntary work for retired or redundant professional and business people.

Bear Wharf
27 Bankside
London SE1 9ET
Tel: 0171-928 0452

RSVP
Arranges projects for older volunteers in local communities.

237 Pentonville Road
London N1 9NJ
Tel: 0171-278 6601

SCORE (Scottish Corps of Retired Executives)
Transfers the expertise of retired business and professional people in Scotland to voluntary organisations, and provides help for emerging small businesses.

43 Station Road
Edinburgh EH12 7AF
Tel: 0131-334 9876

Third Age Challenge Trust
Provides employment-related services to older people.

St James's Walk
Clerkenwell Green
London ECIR OBE
Tel: 0171-336 7477

APPENDIX 4: REFERENCES

All published in London unless otherwise stated.

Action: Employees in the Community (1994) *The Business Case: A briefing paper*.

Action: Employees in the Community (1994) *Business on Board: Support for employees serving on not-for-profit governing bodies*.

Anderson R (1995) *Training Developments and Needs of Older Workers*, European Foundation for the Improvement of Living and Working Conditions, Dublin.

Atkinson J, Meager N, *New Forms of Work Organisation*, Institute of Manpower Studies, (now Institute of Employment Studies).

Berry-Lound D J (1992) *Is Retirement Working?* Help the Aged.

Brewster C et al (1993) *Flexible Working Patterns in Europe*, Institute of Personnel Management.

Carers in Employment Group (1995) *Carers in Employment*, Princess Royal Trust for Carers.

Carnegie UK Trust (1993) *Life, Work and Livelihood in the Third Age: The Report of the Carnegie Inquiry into the Third Age*.

Commission on Social Justice (1994) *Social Justice: Strategies for national renewal*, report of the Commission on Social Justice, Vintage.

Crossroads (1993) *Looking Forward to Looking After*.

Department of Employment (1994) *Getting On*.

Department of Employment (1995) *A Manager's Guide to Teleworking*.

Department of Employment (1995) *Too Old . . . Who says?*

Downs S, Clarke A (1991) *Training Requirements of the Older Worker*, research report for the Department of Employment.

Employment Department Group (1994) *Getting On: The benefits of an older workforce.*

Employment Department Group (1995) *Too Old – who says – advice for older workers.*

Handy C (1989) *The Age of Unreason*, Hutchinson.

Handy C (1994) *The Empty Raincoat*, Hutchinson.

Hutton W (1995) *The State We're In*, Jonathan Cape.

Institute of Personnel Management (now Institute of Personnel and Development) (1993) *Age and Employment: Policies, attitude and practice.*

Institute of Personnel Management (1993) *Statement on Age and Employment.*

Lantrua M, Jones R (1994) *Study of Age Restrictions on Employment Service Vacancies*, Employment Service.

McGoldrick A, Arrowsmith J (1994) *The Employment of Older Workers in the 1990s*, Manchester Metropolitan University.

Metropolitan Recruitment Agency (METRA) (1994) *Lifting the Age Barrier: A practical guide.*

Moore J, Tilson B, Whitting G (1994) *An International Overview of Employment Policies and Practices towards Older Workers*, ECOTEC for the Department of Employment; Research Series No 29.

Naylor P (1990) *Age No Barrier*, Metropolitan Recruitment Agency (METRA).

O'Meara D (1989) *Protecting the Growing Number of Older Workers: The Age Discrimination in Employment Act*, University of Pennsylvania Press.

Parsons D (1987) *Defining the Demographic Time Bomb*, National Economic Development Office.

Peters T (1992) *Liberation Management*, Knopf, New York.

Population Projections 1962-2062, Government Actuary's Department.

Schuller T, Bostyn A M (1992) *Education, Training and Information in the Third Age*, Research Paper No 3 for the Carnegie Inquiry into the Third Age, Carnegie UK Trust.

Social Trends 1995, Central Statistical Office.

Taylor P, Walker A (1993) 'Employers and Older Workers', *Employment Gazette*, on research among employers carried out in 1991.

Taylor P, Walker A (1994) 'The Ageing Workforce: Employers' attitudes towards older workers', *Work, Employment and Society*, Vol 8, No 3.

Taylor P, Walker A (1995) 'Utilising Older Workers', *Employment Gazette*, April 1995.

Thompson M (1991) *Last in the Queue? Corporate employment policies and the older worker* (IMS Report No 09), Institute of Manpower Studies (now Institute of Employment Studies).

Trades Union Congress (1995) *Age Discrimination: Guidance notes for trade unions*.

Trinder C, Hulme G, McCarthy U (1992) *Employment: The role of work in the Third Age*, Research Paper No 1 for the Carnegie Inquiry into the Third Age, Carnegie UK Trust.

US Congress (1993) *Developments in Ageing*, Report of the Special Committee on Ageing, US Senate, Washington DC.

US Department of Labor (1989) *Labor Market Problems of Older Workers*, Report of the Secretary of Labor.

Walker A (1994) *Investing in Ageing Workers: A framework for analysing good practice in Europe*.

Walker J (1992) *Preparing for Retirement: The employer's guide*, Pre-Retirement Association and ACE Books.

World Labour Report 1995, International Labour Organisation, Geneva.

ABOUT AGE CONCERN

Age and Employment: Why employers should think again about older workers is one of a wide range of publications produced by Age Concern England, the National Council on Ageing. Age Concern England is actively engaged in training, information provision, fundraising and campaigning for retired people and those who work with them, and also in the provision of products and services such as insurance for older people.

A network of over 1,400 local Age Concern groups, with the support of around 250,000 volunteers, aims to improve the quality of life for older people and develop services appropriate to local needs and resources. These include advice and information, day care, visiting services, transport schemes, clubs, and specialist facilities for older people who are physically and mentally frail.

Age Concern England is a registered charity dependent on public support for the continuation and development of its work.

Age Concern England
1268 London Road
London SW16 4ER
Tel: 0181-679 8000

Age Concern Scotland
113 Rose Street
Edinburgh EH2 3DT
Tel: 0131-220 3345

Age Concern Cymru
4th Floor
1 Cathedral Road
Cardiff CF1 9SD
Tel: 01222 371566

Age Concern Northern Ireland
3 Lower Crescent
Belfast BT7 1NR
Tel: 01232 245729

PUBLICATIONS FROM ◆A◆C◆E◆ BOOKS

A wide range of titles is published by Age Concern England under the ACE Books imprint.

Employment

Preparing for Retirement: The employer's guide
Joanna Walker

The need to prepare staff for their retirement is widely accepted, yet many organisations fail to provide any training at all. This guide, designed to help personnel staff formulate a pre-retirement training policy, sets out the options available and the stages that need to be followed.

Co-published with the Pre-Retirement Association

£12.95   0-86242-068-7

Changing Direction: Employment options in mid-life
Sue Ward

Redundancy or early retirement can come as a shock to anyone, but the impact in mid-life can be devastating. This topical and highly practical book is designed to help those aged 40-55 get back to work, examining issues such as adjusting to change, your finances, opportunities for work, deciding what work you really want to do, looking for a job and working for yourself.

£6.95   0-86242-190-X

Earning Money in Retirement
Kenneth Lysons
Many people, for a variety of reasons, wish to continue in some form of paid employment after they have retired. This helpful guide explores the practical implications of such a choice and highlights some of the opportunities available.
£5.95   0-86242-103-9

Retirement

An Active Retirement
Nancy Tuft
Packed with information on hobbies, sports, educational opportunities and voluntary work, this practical guide is ideal for retired people seeking new ways to fill their time but uncertain where to start.
£7.95   0-86242-119-5

Your Retirement
Caroline Hartnell
A comprehensive handbook for older people leaving employment and looking ahead to retirement. Full of practical advice to assist with planning and adjustment, topics covered include: managing money, using your time, staying healthy, housing and special needs.
£4.95   0-86242-144-6

If you would like to order any of these titles, please write to the address below, enclosing a cheque or money order for the appropriate amount made payable to Age Concern England. Credit card orders may be made on 0181-679 8000.

Mail Order Unit
Age Concern England
PO Box 9
London SW16 4EX

INDEX